Barbara

D1141414

Barbara

PERSPECTIVE FOR ARTISTS

PERSPECTIVE
FOR ARTISTS

ANGELA GAIR

ARTISTS HOUSE

Design	Hans Verkroost
Editor	Alison Franks
Production	Peter Philips,
	Sarah Schuman

Mitchell Beazley Publishers, Michelin House
81 Fulham Road, London SW3 6RB.

Copyright © 1990 Mitchell Beazley Publishers
Text copyright © 1990 Angela Gair
Reprinted 1992

All rights reserved. No part of this work may be
reproduced or utilized in any form or by any means,
electronic or mechanical, including photocopying,
recording or by any information storage and retrieval
systems, without the prior written permission of the publishers.

The publishers have made every effort to ensure that all
instructions given in this book are accurate and safe,
but they cannot accept liability for any injury, damage or loss
to either person or property whether direct or consequential
and howsoever arising. The author and publishers will be
grateful for any information which will assist them in keeping
future editions up to date.

ISBN 1-85732-963-5

Typeset by Hourds Typographica, Stafford.
Origination by La Cromolito s.n.c., Milan.
Produced by Mandarin Offset.
Printed in Hong Kong

CONTENTS

INTRODUCTION

It is said that the great Renaissance painter Paolo Uccello used to wake up in the night and cry, "Oh, my dear wife, how beautiful perspective is!" Now, that may sound a touch ironic to those of you who are currently wrestling with the problems of perspective and wondering why the buildings in your painting look as if they're about to keel over, or why the sky in your landscape looks like a flat wall behind the scene instead of receding into the distance.

But take heart; perspective is indeed beautiful. For, once the basic principles have been learned, you will find that it helps you to draw much more confidently, while also opening up a whole new field of exciting and previously unexplored subject matter.

I sometimes think it is the term "perspective" itself which puts people off, since it is a rather cold, antiseptic word that has connotations of geometry, mathematics and other apparently

soulless activities. However, drawing in perspective is the only means we have at our disposal for representing three-dimensional space on a two-dimensional surface, so it is a discipline that cannot be avoided.

Learning to draw objects in perspective is like learning to drive a car; there may be a few bumps and jolts and false starts at first, but after a while everything suddenly clicks into place and you can breeze along with confidence. I'll never forget when I first learned how to draw in perspective a bridge supported on a series of arches, receding into the distance. I couldn't believe it could be so simple, and yet look

so credible, and since I had always come bottom of the class at school in mathematics and geometry, my sense of pride and achievement was doubly satisfying!

In the following chapters, I will touch on the general rules of perspective that are essential to all artists, and show how these rules can be applied to a wide range of painting subjects: landscapes, townscapes, still life, interiors and figures. With the aid of easy-to-follow text, step-by-step demonstrations and finished examples by practising artists, I have tried to approach perspective in a way that's logical and simple, and relevant to you as a painter. Technical books on perspective are crammed with mathematical formulae and fearsomely complicated diagrams bristling with perspective lines. They are fine for architects and draughtsmen, but for most artists a firm grasp of the basic rules, coupled with direct and keen observation, are all that's required to enable you to create a convincing sense of three-dimensional space in your pictures. Indeed, the "ruler and compass" approach to perspective is inappropriate in painting; a mechanically perfect rendering can lack sensitivity and appear tight and rigid, whereas freely drawn lines, even if they are slightly less accurate, give character and life to a picture.

I should add here, however, that I am not advocating poor or lazy drawing. The student of art *must* practise his or her drawing skills seriously and often; contrary to popular belief, talented artists are made and not born, and they have to work hard in order to achieve their goals. After all, who would expect a musician to play a Beethoven concerto who had not first learned to read music or practised his or her technique to perfection?

The fundamentals of perspective are not dificult to grasp; with a little practice and application, and with this book to help you, I believe that drawing in perspective will have you hooked in no time.

HISTORY AND BACKGROUND

Over the centuries, artists have used widely differing conventions of perspective with which to record their perceptions of the world around them. Civilizations have come and gone, and it can be useful and enlightening for the modern artist to learn how each has evolved an artistic style that reflects the period's attitudes and ideologies.

Since the 16th century, achieving a sense of realism in a painting or drawing has been one of the most challenging and highly regarded aspects of representing the natural world. But it was not always so. The Ancient Egyptians, for example, were not concerned with "realism" as we define it today; their painting and sculpture served a religious, rather than a purely decorative, purpose. The Egyptians believed in the afterlife, and pharaohs and noblemen were regarded as divine beings who, after death, moved on to another life among the gods. Their tombs were adorned with images of their family and servants, and of animals, birds, trees, fields and water. These images were believed to provide the soul of the dead ruler with all he would need in the afterlife — rather as if he were embarking on a long journey.

It was important that these images were accurate, so that everything would be preserved permanently and completely in the world beyond. The artist was not concerned with representing objects as seen from a particular angle at a given moment in time: instead, he combined both frontal and profile views of objects so that they would be instantly recognizable to the spirits in the hereafter. Figures were portrayed with the head in profile, but with the eye painted as though viewed from the front. The body was seen straight on, but with the limbs viewed in profile. Foreshortening was avoided, as it would distort the image and make it less easily recognizable.

The paintings and sculptures of Ancient Greece and Rome expressed a love of order and harmony and a belief in the inherent beauty of the human form. Artists began to make much more realistic representations of the human figure; the discovery of foreshortening, in 500BC, enabled them to draw a foot, for example, as seen from in front.

After the decline of the Roman Empire in the 5th century, the Christian church became the most important patron of art in western Europe. Once again, artists were required to paint within strict guidelines founded in religious belief. Only certain ways of depicting the figure and facial expressions were permitted, and Greek naturalism gave way to flat, two-dimensional images which were highly stylized and richly

Above: Raphael Sanzio's fresco *The School of Athens* is considered to be one of the greatest spatial compositions of all time.

Right: The Dutch painters of the 17th century were masters of landscape composition. In Philips Koninck's *An Extensive Landscape with a Road by a River* the low horizon gives prominence to the vast sky. The winding curves of the road and river lead the eye back into the picture towards the horizon.

During the 15th century there was great demand for books illustrated with scenes from contemporary life. *The Month of February*, **left**, is a page from the *Book of Hours* painted by the Limbourg brothers. In an effort to give the picture depth, the artists used converging lines in buildings and painted figures smaller as they recede into the distance.

Vilhelm Hammershoi was a Danish artist painting at the turn of the 19th century. In *Interior with Seated Woman*, **above**, the composition and perspective are carefully structured to enhance the mood of quiet contemplation.

Above: Canaletto's early training as a scene painter influenced the way he constructed his paintings. *Regatta on the Grand Canal* is typical of his grand vistas of Venice, with elaborate architecture seen in sharp perspective and with the vanishing point just off centre.

ornamented. Almost all paintings depicted religious scenes, intended as visual stories for the illiterate masses, and landscape was relegated to a mere backdrop against which the main action took place. Although a limited knowledge of perspective and anatomy existed, it was considered unimportant, since the symbolic and narrative content of pictures took precedence over descriptive realism.

By the 14th century, a gradual evolution towards the realistic representation of space and form had begun. Although the fundamental principles of perspective were not yet fully understood, nevertheless painters such as Giotto (*c.*1267–1337) and Gentile de Fabriano became increasingly interested in the representation of three-dimensional figures placed in a defined space. The emphasis in painting was changing from religion towards realism, with artists working from direct observation and using light and shade to model forms in the round. There was a growing interest in portrait painting and in landscapes depicting scenes from contemporary life. In an effort to give their landscapes depth, artists used converging lines in buildings and painted figures in the distance smaller than those in the foreground.

However, it wasn't until the time of the Renaissance, in the 15th century, that artists were able to achieve a systematic means of representing space in pictures. The term Renaissance means "rebirth", and the 15th and 16th centuries witnessed an extraordinary period of exploration and discovery in the fields of science, philosophy and the visual arts. The great Florentine architect and mathematician Filippo Brunelleschi (1377–1446) pioneered a system of mathematical laws governing perspective and the art of suggesting depth on a flat two-dimensional surface. The techniques he devised to render objects diminishing with distance revolutionized painting and are still used by western artists today. Brunelleschi established that there must be a fixed horizon line, and that horizontal lines running away from the observer into the distance, although parallel in reality, appear to converge towards a single vanishing point on the horizon line. The principles of perspective were put into effect by other Renaissance painters, including Paolo Uccello (1397–1475), Piero della Francesca (1420–1492) and Leon Battista Alberti (1404–1472). Leonardo da Vinci (1452–1519), in his *Treatise on Painting*, wrote at length about the phenomenon of atmospheric perspective, where objects in the distance appear paler in tone and bluer in hue because of the effect of the intervening atmosphere.

During the 17th century, landscape painting at last came into its own. Private patronage had begun to replace that of the Church, and artists were freer to paint what interested them. Nature became a major theme in paintings, and the suggestion of space and depth within a picture was achieved by means of atmospheric perspective. By the use of warm browns in the foreground, shades of green in the middle distance and pale blues in the far distance, the eye was encouraged to travel back and long distances could be suggested in this way. The

greatest exponents of this type of painting were the Flemish artists such as Meindert Hobbema (1638–1709), Jacob van Ruisdael (1628–1682) and Peter Paul Rubens (1577–1640), whose canvases often depicted huge, dramatic skies and wide views of rolling countryside stretching far back to the horizon.

The Flemish style of painting influenced many English painters, among them John Sell Cotman (1782–1842), Thomas Gainsborough (1727–1788) and John Constable (1776–1837), all of whom painted nature "in the raw" and were fascinated by the effects of light and shade, clouds and sunlight. Joseph Mallord William Turner (1775–1851), who was, incidentally, the first Professor of Perspective at the Royal Academy in London, inspired artists throughout Europe with his passion for colour and light. His later landscape paintings reveal a world of infinite space, filled with air and light, and were a significant influence in the development of French Impressionism.

The 20th century has seen a great many changes in artistic style and expression,

reflecting perhaps the uncertainty of modern society's ideals and aspirations. It is as if, having learned all there is to learn about perspective, painters now want to extend the boundaries of realism and break all the accepted conventions. Nevertheless, artists have continued to draw and paint in more traditional ways, and the desire to suggest three-dimensional space in pictures will surely remain a fundamental impulse for every artist.

Below: *Norham Castle* was painted towards the end of Turner's life and reflects his obsession with the effects of light and atmosphere on the landscape. A haze of diffused brilliance almost obliterates the distant castle and trees, evoking a sense of infinite space. At the time, pictures like this attracted much criticism, but Turner was unrepentant. "Indistinctness," he once said to a complaining client, "is my forté."

WORKING WITH PERSPECTIVE

Most paintings and drawings – realistic ones at least – contain clues which help the viewer to visualize the size, shape and volume of the objects in the original scene, and the distance between them. It is perspective that gives this impression of a third dimension and adds realism to a drawn or painted image. This chapter begins by exploring some of the simple, familiar methods which artists use to achieve a sense of three-dimensional space in paintings and drawings. Converging lines, overlapping forms and diminishing scale, are just some of the compositional devices that can be used to trick the eye into believing that some areas of the picture are nearer than others. It then goes on to explain the basic principles of linear perspective, by which you can learn to draw a subject from any angle, confident in the knowledge that it will appear solid, three-dimensional and believable.

This watercolour painting by Ronald Jesty demonstrates how a firm grasp of perspective can open up a wealth of possibilities for dynamic composition.

EMPHASIZING DEPTH

Long before the rules of linear perspective were formulated, artists knew how to create depth in a picture by using optical illusions to trick the eye into believing some parts of the scene are closer than other parts. By choosing the right viewpoint, or arranging objects in a certain way, it is possible to encourage the eye to move from one part of the picture to another and entice it toward the background, thus heightening the experience of spatial depth.

Using Scale

Scale – the size of objects relative to one another and to you, the observer – has a vital role to play in any painting or drawing. The ability to reflect scale effectively not only establishes the relationships between different parts of a scene, but also reveals information about the spaces between them, and this in turn draws the eye into the picture.

In everyday life, we use, quite unconsciously, the scale of the objects around us to help judge where we stand in relation to our surroundings. For example, try looking at a chair on the far side of a room, then compare its size with that of a cup held in front of your eyes; although the cup is the smaller of the two objects, it appears larger because it is nearer and your brain uses this information to judge how far away from the chair you are standing.

When composing a painting or drawing, try introducing contrasts of scale in the arrangement so as to create depth. If all the objects in the picture are of the same size, or on the same visual plane, it removes any sense of space or distance and causes the scene to look flat and uninteresting. The trick is to use scale as a means of establishing the foreground, middle ground and background.

Left: Setting the scale of a picture works best if the objects within it are of a "known" size in real life. For this reason, figures make the best "scale setters": depending on the size they appear in the picture, our minds (which know what size they really are) instinctively build the rest of the scene around them. Here, the great difference in scale between the large foreground figure and the tiny background figures and trees suggests the spaciousness of the park and at the same time creates a visually arresting composition.
Far left: In this street scene, notice how the scale is "set" by the figures in the immediate foreground and how the progressive reduction in size of the figures and vehicles leads the eye down the street. Lines and details become looser and less distinct towards the background, which accentuates the effect of distance.

Above: Space and three-dimension are as important in still life painting as they are in landscapes. Here Geoff Humphreys has arranged vases of flowers and a jug against the receding plane of the table. The overlapping shapes and colours lead the eye around the composition and generate visual energy.

Overlapping forms

Another effective way of creating the illusion of three-dimensional space is by overlapping elements in a picture. When two shapes overlap, the eye perceives one as being behind the other and so further from the eye. Even when the objects are of the same size, the eye tends to accept a condition of depth when one overlaps the other. When overlapping and dimunition of size are combined in a picture, an even stronger suggestion of space is created.

Converging lines

Parallel horizontal lines that recede into the distance, such as roads, fences, railway tracks and lines of telegraph poles, will appear to converge as they approach the horizon. In a composition, lines sloping inward from the edges of the picture and travelling from the foreground to the mid- or far distance can give a dynamic sense of depth. This phenomenon is the basis for linear perspective, discussed in more detail later in this chapter.

Using a grid

With the aid of a simple grid you can quickly learn how perspective works in street scenes and landscapes. Take a piece of transparent acetate or tracing paper and with a biro or pencil draw a grid of 5mm ($\frac{1}{2}$in) or 10mm (1in) squares on it (see **right**). Place the grid over a photograph of a street with buildings receding into the distance. You will be able to see — because your grid has equal squares — how objects steadily become smaller, narrower and more closely spaced as they recede from view.

Left: The composition of this landscape by Lucy Willis encourages the eye to move around the picture, just as it would when viewing a real landscape. The diagonal line of the trees leads us down the hill to the fields. From there the winding road leads us up the hill to the group of buildings which, in turn, direct us back to the trees.

Below: The receding lines of the paving stones, fence, windows and roofs combine to create a diagonal view across the picture, leading the eye back into the distance.

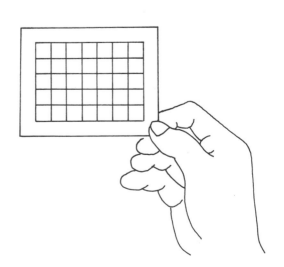

LINEAR PERSPECTIVE

Every object around us, from a soup can to a skyscraper, has a form based on geometry. Even the organic forms of nature can be broken down and simplified into cubes, spheres, cones and cylinders. To draw objects in perspective, therefore, requires a basic knowledge of geometry; this helps us to understand the way in which shapes apparently change and become distorted, depending on the angle they are viewed from.

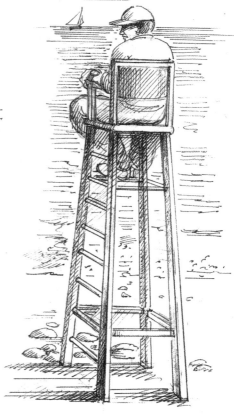

Above: These three drawings show how when you move from a low viewpoint to a high one the horizon line always corresponds to your eye level. The horizon moves up with you and your area of vision is extended.

Below: If you can't see the actual horizon of the scene you are drawing or painting, hold a pencil horizontally about 12" (30cm) in front of your eyes. Imagine a line extending from the pencil in both directions and that is your horizon.

The rules of perspective exist to make our rendering of three-dimensional space on a flat surface such as paper accurate and plausible. Such rules may be very important to the architect and the technical draughtsman, but for artists they should serve only as guidelines: an over-preoccupation with perspective can have an inhibiting effect, and can give your drawings a sterile, mechanical appearance.

A general grasp of perspective, coupled with good observation, is enough for most working artists. What follows, then, are the basic principles, which will enable you confidently to sketch and paint any subject you might come across, from a chair to a city street.

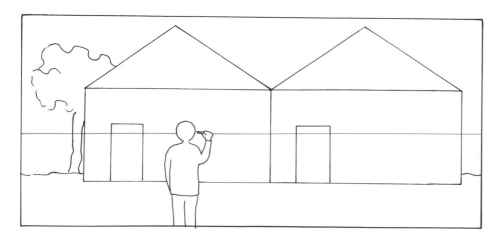

The horizon line

Before you can draw anything in perspective, you must first establish the horizon line, or eye level. We all know that the horizon is the point at which the earth — or the sea — and the sky meet. But remember that the horizon is not fixed and immovable: if you stand on the beach and face the ocean, without raising or lowering your head, the horizon is directly in line with your gaze. If you climb to the top of a high cliff and look out at the ocean, again you will find that the horizon is in line with your gaze — you will not be looking down on it. In other words, the position of the horizon *always* corresponds with the eye level of the observer. This point is especially relevant to the artist drawing a scene in perspective — it is vital to establish the correct position of the horizon because, as we shall discover shortly, all parallel horizontal lines that run away from you into the distance appear to converge at a point on the horizon line.

Quite often, our view of the horizon is hidden by buildings, trees and so on. In such cases, it is an easy matter to gauge the position of the horizon line; hold a pencil horizontally at arm's length, level with your eyes, and note at what height it comes in relation to the scene before you. Lightly draw a line at the relevant position on your paper, this is the line on which you will plot the *vanishing point*. If you are looking at a subject directly from above or below, the horizon might well be outside the edges of the picture. In this case you must imagine the location of the horizon line and vanishing points and estimate the angles of the converging lines.

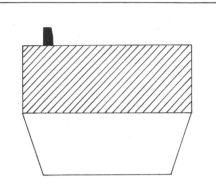

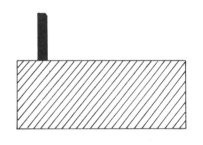

Far left: If an object is above eye level, the bottom of the object is visible. If the object is divided by the horizon line, neither the top nor the bottom is visible. If the object is below the horizon line, the top side is visible.

Above: Here the road dips downward, therefore the parallel lines of the road and the low wall on the right appear to converge at a point below the horizon line. The houses, however, are built on level foundations, therefore the horizontal lines of roofs, walls and windows converge toward the horizon line.

Left: The buildings in the background are above the horizon line, therefore their roofs are not visible.

Above: To emphasize the height of the buildings, David Curtis has chosen a low viewpoint for this city street scene. As the horizon line is near the bottom of the picture, the parallel lines of the tops of the buildings appear to converge downward; this "throws" the eye from foreground to background, adding to the dramatic sense of scale and depth.

Right: In this painting the high horizon line draws the eye down into the quiet seclusion of the scene.

Horizon line

Above: The horizon line is above the picture area and eliminates the sky completely, focusing attention on a small detail of the scene. This has produced a picture with a confined and intimate atmosphere.

Left: It is best to avoid a centrally placed horizon line, as this tends to create a static and symmetrical composition; it is more effective to place it either above or below the centre of the picture. Here, the horizon line is slightly above centre, putting the emphasis on the curve of the farm track which leads our eye from the front of the picture to the distant figures.

Vanishing points

Having established the horizon line, the next point to recognize is that all parallel horizontal lines that recede into the distance appear to converge toward the horizon line. Receding parallel lines above eye level, like the tops of buildings, appear to slant downward toward the horizon line. All lines below eye level, such as railway tracks, roads, fences and so on, slant upward toward the horizon line. Vertical lines, however, remain vertical (unless they are viewed from an extreme high or low viewpoint) because they maintain the same distance from the observer throughout their length.

All parallel horizontal lines going back into space will appear to move closer to each other, finally converging at a point somewhere on the horizon line. This is known as the *vanishing point*. The vanishing point gives you an exact method for determining the angle of every receding line in your picture, thus ensuring that your drawings are accurate and true.

Depending on the position of the subject in relation to the artist, there might be one, two, or even several vanishing points in one picture. The examples on the following pages will demonstrate why this is so. You can test these theories for yourself by holding a small box at eye level and observing what happens as you move it through different angles.

Above: Drawing a room or corridor is an excellent way of discovering how one-point perspective works. Note here how the square tiles on the floor appear smaller and closer together as they recede from the eye.

Right: This pen and ink drawing uses the effect of perspective to great advantage. The dynamic lines of the walls disappearing into the distance help to convey a sense of the imposing size of the cathedral.

One-point perspective
To practise rendering objects in one-point perspective it is helpful to begin by drawing a square or rectangular box.

1 First draw the vertical line of the side of the box nearest to you.

2 Estimate the angle of slope of the top and bottom lines (red) of the receding side of the box. Draw the horizon line (blue) through the vanishing point.

3 Draw the side of the box which is parallel to the picture plane.

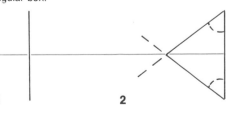
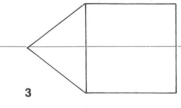
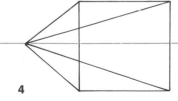

1   2   3   4

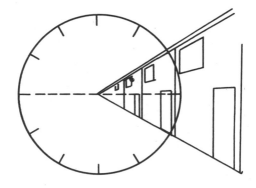

When estimating the angles of perspective lines, a helpful trick is to imagine a clock face centred on the horizon line, with the vanishing point at its centre. You can "read" the angles of the buildings as you would the time.

Right: These boxes demonstrate the principle of one-point perspective: that all parallel horizontal lines meet at eye level and that the side planes of objects appear smaller and closer together the further they are from the eye.

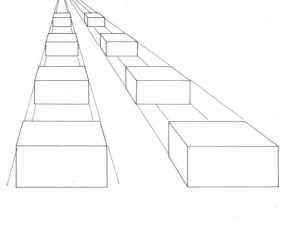

One-point perspective

The centre line of vision is an imaginary perpendicular line which is drawn from the artist's position to the horizon line, meeting it at right angles. If you are looking at a subject directly in line with your line of vision (say you are standing in the middle of a street, with buildings on either side, looking toward the far end of the street, then all lines which move away from you will appear to converge at dead centre – the point on the horizon line where your line of vision strikes it. This is the most simple form of perspective, known as one-point or parallel perspective because all parallel lines converge at a single point.

If you are standing on one side of the street, facing at an angle to the buildings opposite, then the receding parallel lines will not be in line with your line of vision, and neither will the vanishing point. To locate the vanishing point, take a pencil or ruler and, holding it before your eyes as level as possible, estimate by comparison with this horizontal the angle of slope of the top of the building. Having obtained the slope of your top line, all you have to do is to extend this line to the horizon line.

Next, estimate the height of the nearest upright: it might be the corner of the nearest building, or a doorway. You can now draw the bottom line of the building, from the base of the upright to the point on the horizon line at which the top line intersected. Having established the vanishing point, it is an easy matter to draw the lines of windows, doors and so on in the same perspective.

Below: The geometry of the perspective lines in this composition is softened by the dappled shadows and by the curve of the path in the foreground.

4 To establish the receding planes of the far side of the box, draw lines connecting the top and bottom corners to the vanishing point (red).

5 Estimate the width of the nearside of the box and draw a vertical line at the back. Complete the back side of the box as shown.

6 Erase all working lines to reveal a view of the inside of the box.

7 By erasing all the lines inside the box, you are left with an exterior view of the box.

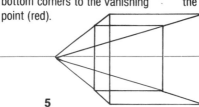

5

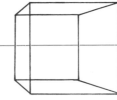

6

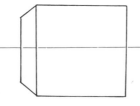

7

Two-point perspective

When we look at objects from an oblique angle rather than straight on we get a very different view of things. Standing diagonally opposite the corner of a building, for example, our centre line of vision is directed at the point where the corner vertically cuts the horizon. There are no lines here parallel to the artist's point of vision:

instead there are two sets of receding parallel lines, each of which runs toward its own vanishing point on the horizon. This is known as two-point or angular perspective.

When two-point perspective is involved, it is likely that at least one vanishing point, and sometimes both, will be outside the picture area. You have to imagine the vanishing points in the

space beyond your page, and estimate the angles of buildings and so on by eye. Don't worry if the angles you draw are less than accurate at first, just keep practising. Train your eye to judge angles and distances, learn to trust your own judgement and pretty soon you'll be able to sketch any subject without relying on eye level and vanishing point at all.

1 Plot the position of the horizon line on the paper. Then plot the position and height of the vertical nearest to the picture plane.
2 Find the angles of the top and

bottom of the receding plane on one side of the vertical. Extend these lines so they meet at the horizon line. This gives you the first vanishing point.

3 Find the angle of the top of the receding plane on the other side of the vertical and extend the line to the horizon as before.
4 Do the same with the bottom of

the receding plane and establish the second vanishing point.
5 Estimate the width of the two side planes and draw in the verticals at the far corners.

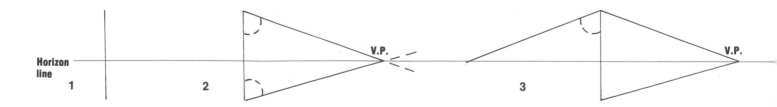

Step 1

Step 2

Step 3

Left: Good compositions are all around us if we open our eyes and look. Lucy Willis painted this charmingly informal scene in her back garden. The empty chairs, arranged at different angles, created bold white shapes which made an interesting contrast with the organic forms of the garden.

The three steps **above** show how she approached the painting. In step 1, the main outlines are drawn in pencil, with the chairs in two-point perspective. The white shapes of the chairs are indicated by painting the dark foliage behind them.

In step 2, more darks and cast shadows are indicated. When painting outdoors, these may change a lot before the painting is completed, so it's important to get them consistent at the beginning. In step 3, the lighter greens of the grass and foliage are brushed in, working around the white shapes of the chairs and foreground flowers. In the final stage (see **left**) the dark tones are strengthened and the figure, tree and flowers are completed.

Above: When it comes to emphasizing the three-dimensional quality of a subject, two vanishing points are better than one. To paint this building, for example, Lucy Willis positioned herself in front of the point where two walls meet, so that both are seen at an angle. This gives a greater sense of depth than a head-on view of one side of the house. In addition, one side of the house is in shadow and the other side is lit, thus conveying the volume and solidity of the structure.

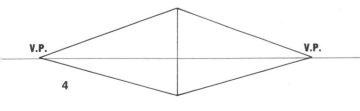

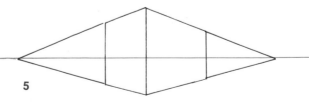

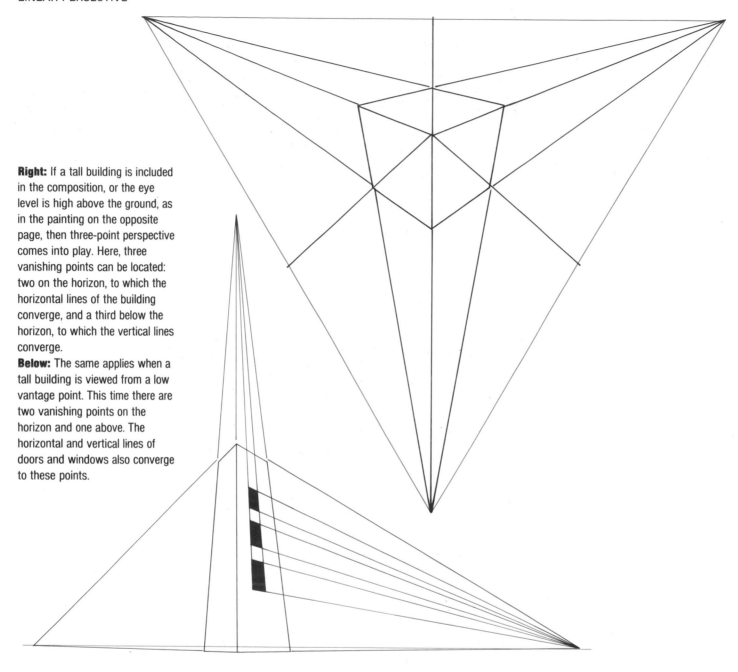

Right: If a tall building is included in the composition, or the eye level is high above the ground, as in the painting on the opposite page, then three-point perspective comes into play. Here, three vanishing points can be located: two on the horizon, to which the horizontal lines of the building converge, and a third below the horizon, to which the vertical lines converge.

Below: The same applies when a tall building is viewed from a low vantage point. This time there are two vanishing points on the horizon and one above. The horizontal and vertical lines of doors and windows also converge to these points.

Three-point perspective

1 Find the vertical line closest to you, then find the angle of the top of a receding plane. Extend this line (red) to the horizon (blue).

2 Draw a line from the base of the vertical to the horizon line, as shown. The point where the two lines meet is the vanishing point.

3 Repeat this process to establish the other vanishing point on the horizon line (blue).

4 To find the vertical vanishing point, first estimate the width of each side of the cube and the angle of the receding verticals. The vertical vanishing point is the point at which these vertical angles intersect on a line perpendicular to the horizon line.

1

2

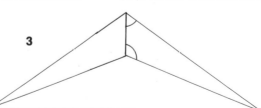

3

Three-point perspective

So far we've considered a perspective view of things that are looked at straight on. In such cases only the horizontal lines appear to converge while all the vertical lines remain parallel and vertical. But what happens when we look up at a tall building, for instance, or look down from a high window at the street below?

As we look up at a building from a low viewpoint, the parallel sides appear to recede from us, so they will eventually converge at a point *above* the building. This requires an extra vanishing point in addition to the one or two vanishing points on the horizon. The same thing happens when we look down at objects and the extra vanishing point is located *below* it.

This is called three-point or oblique perspective.

Multiple vanishing points

Objects placed at different angles to the picture plane, as in the case of a street scene viewed from above, may have multiple vanishing points. Attempting to plot the exact location of all these vanishing points is neither necessary nor desirable. It is enough simply to observe the angles and convergences, checking their accuracy as you go along by comparing one with another and with the horizontal of your eye level. Often, any small inaccuracies will add to the character of, say, a group of ramshackle rooftops in an old town.

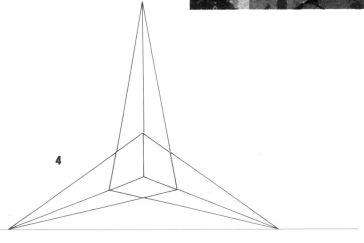

4

Above: For this rooftop view of an Italian town, Ronald Jesty juggled with the viewpoint until he found the most effective combination of colours, perspective and play of light and shade. Follow the lines of the buildings and you will see that each converges at a different vanishing point on the horizon, because each is facing at a different angle.

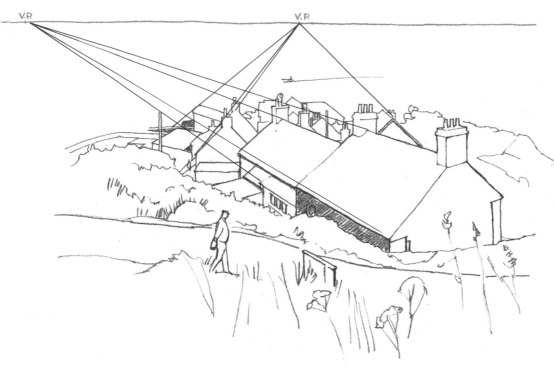

Artist Ronald Jesty was attracted to this scene because of its unusual perspective. He found a comfortable spot on the hillside above the village, looking out over the rooftops and the sea to the distant horizon, and began by making several sketches of the buildings. In his initial charcoal sketch (**above**) he checked that the perspective of the buildings was correct by extending the lines of the rooftops to their respective vanishing points on the horizon. He then made a working drawing in ink (**below**) based on the first sketch but including more detail. Finally he painted the scene in watercolour (**right**). Notice how the artist uses the diminishing scale of the foreground grasses, the figure, the buildings and the tiny fishing boat to direct our gaze to the distant horizon.

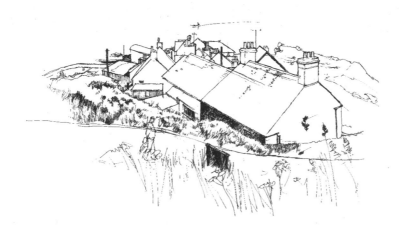

USING LIGHT AND SHADE

The previous chapter discussed the various *linear* methods of creating the illusion of form and space on a two-dimensional surface. But these alone do not tell the full story. Another vital component in our box of visual tricks is the use of light and shade.

The way light falls on an object tells us much about its form and solidity. But certain kinds of light define form more clearly than others because they create a more descriptive pattern of light and shadow. When the sun is shining from directly behind you onto the landscape, the features of the land may appear somewhat flattened and there will be a lack of tonal contrast due to the general absence of shadow. This is fine if you wish to accentuate pattern and colour, but not if you want to convey a realistic impression of depth and form. On the other hand, when light falls on the subject from

Opposite page: Compare these two sketches and notice how important the shadows and cast shadows are in defining the forms.
Below: The subject of this painting by Lucy Willis is the long shadows cast by trees on the right. Snaking across the track and up through the corn, the shadows vividly describe the contours of the land.
Below right: In hard directional light – midday sunlight, for example – the patterns of lights and shadows can become more powerful than the subject. Hazel Harrison painted this scene in Greece.
Right: The length of cast shadows depends on the height of the sun. When the sun is at a 45° angle, the shadow cast is the same length as the height of the object casting it (**A**). When the sun is high the shadow is short (**B**); when it is low the shadow is long (**C**).

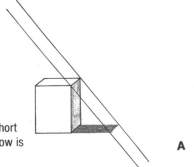

A

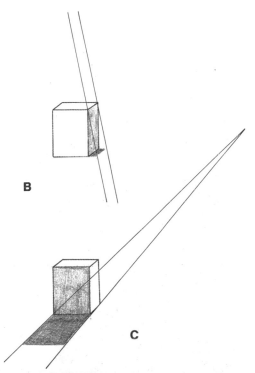

B

C

an angle of 45° or so, a strong impression of form and depth is given because there is a good balance of light and shadow that describes the contours. In addition, the shadows cast by trees and so on help to define the contours of the ground on which they fall. Shadows are also vital compositional elements, creating interesting shapes and tonal patterns that keep the eye moving around the picture.

Cast shadows

The shadow cast by an object onto the ground plane helps to define the object's position in space and its relation to other objects around it. It is important, therefore, that cast shadows are drawn correctly in relation to the objects casting them and to the light source.

The rays of the sun are considered to be parallel, and they strike the ground obliquely. Since these rays cannot travel around corners or through solid matter, an object in the path of the sun will block out those rays that hit it, causing an absence of light – a shadow – on the opposite side to the direction of the light. The shadow starts at the base of the object and ends with the first light ray that is able to pass directly over it.

The height of the sun determines the length of the shadows (see diagrams **above right**). The position of the sun determines the direction in which the shadows fall; if the sun shines from the west, shadows of objects will lie due east and vice versa.

An important point to remember about shadows produced by the sun is that they are continually moving. It's a good idea to mark the positions of the shadows early on, as they may have altered considerably by the time your drawing or painting is finished.

Tonal contrasts

To emphasize the feeling of distance in your landscape paintings, it is worth noting that areas of light and dark tone can be cunningly arranged and distributed so as to pull the eye through from foreground to middle ground or background. For example, by simplifying and darkening the foreground you will ensure that it doesn't detract from the details in the background. In addition, the contrast between dark tones in the foreground, which, because they are stronger, appear to advance, and lighter tones in the distance, which, being weaker appear to retreat, also emphasizes the illusion of deep space.

Counterchange

Another helpful device for enhancing the depth illusion is counterchange. Essentially, this means the placing of dark shapes against light ones, and light shapes against dark. In a landscape, for instance, a dark tree may be silhouetted against a light sky, a light-toned building in front of a group of dark trees, a dark figure against a light wall, and so on. These light-dark contrasts act as visual "stepping-stones", subtly drawing the viewer's eye through the picture and lending rhythm and movement to the composition.

Left: David Curtis exploits the contrast between the pale, muted tones in the distance and the strong tones in the foreground to heighten the sense of depth in this harbour scene.

Above: More sharply defined contrasts of light shapes against dark, dark shapes against light here set up a rhythm which "pulls" the eye from the foreground to the background.

PERSPECTIVE IN LANDSCAPE

Landscape has perhaps a wider appeal than any other painting subject. Recording the beauty of nature has been a lifetime quest for some artists, who have revelled in the challenge of capturing the transient effects of light and weather on the landscape, and with recreating sometimes vast areas of space on a small, flat piece of paper or canvas. A landscape might incorporate a simple view of a garden or park, or it might encompass fields, woods and hills stretching far into the distance. Whatever the subject, one of the most important considerations in painting a realistic landscape is creating a sense of depth — an illusion of space and distance that invites the viewer to "step into" the picture and stirs the imagination. This chapter explains how to use both linear and atmospheric perspective to convey distance in landscapes. It also pinpoints specific landscape elements, such as sky and water, and explains how they, too, are subject to the laws of perspective.

In this watercolour landscape, Ronald Jesty uses atmospheric perspective and the overlapping shapes of hills and trees to evoke a sense of space and depth.

ATMOSPHERIC PERSPECTIVE

Atmospheric perspective, also called aerial or colour perspective, is a device which has been used for centuries by artists to enhance pictorial depth in landscape compositions. Whereas linear perspective – converging lines, overlapping forms and so on – helps to plot the position of objects in space, atmospheric perspective describes something far less tangible – the effects of light and atmosphere on the visible world.

The term "atmospheric perspective" describes a phenomenon which we've all noticed while out walking in the country: objects which are far off in the distance appear hazier, bluer and lighter in tone than the same objects in the immediate foreground. This is an optical illusion created by nature, caused by the presence of water vapour and particles of dust in the atmosphere. This atmospheric haze intervenes between the observer and the subject and affects our perception of colours, which appear to change according to their distance from our eyes. (You will notice that the effect is more marked on a hazy day.)

To demonstrate the effects of atmospheric perspective more clearly, it helps to imagine the landscape as a series of "stage flats", as shown **opposite**. As our eye moves from foreground to background, these changes take place:
● Tones are strongest in the foreground, becoming progressively weaker in the distance. Tonal contrasts also become weaker: in the foreground, the contrast in tone between the lit side and the shadow side of a tree will be fairly strong, but in the distance light tones appear darker and dark tones appear lighter.
● Colours in the foreground are seen at their fullest intensity, but gradually become more neutral and less intense in the distance, often appearing blue or purple on the horizon.
● The texture, detail and outline of objects are clearly seen in the foreground, but become less distinct the further away they are.

Above: In this painting the colours, tones and details are as strong in the background as they are in the foreground. This makes the background jump forward and lessens the impression of space and recession.

Above right: Here we have the same composition, but the effect of depth and recession is much greater because the strong colours and tones in the foreground come forward while the misty blues in the background appear to recede.

Left and above: A useful tip for representing atmospheric perspective is to visualize the scene as a series of "stage flats". The foreground is strongest in colour, tone and detail; the middle ground and background become progressively paler and less defined.

Far left: On a small sheet of paper Lucy Willis has painted a breathtaking view of the Cotswold countryside. Notice how she divides the composition into three distinct planes going back in space — the strong, dark foreground, the brightly lit middle ground, and the hazy, blue-grey hills in the background.

Top left: Early morning and late afternoon, when the sun is low in the sky, are the best times of the day to observe the effects of atmospheric perspective. In this overhead view of a London dockland development, misty light envelops the buildings and they become hazier and lighter in tone as they recede into the distance. This not only enhances the effect of distance but also adds an air of mystery to the scene which holds the viewer's attention. To achieve this effect in watercolour David Curtis used very wet, fluid washes on a heavy paper.

Above: A striking composition painted by Stephen Darbyshire on the balcony of St Mark's Basilica in Venice. Colour and detail are strongest in the foreground, which has the effect of bringing the statue and figures forward in the picture plane. The buildings on either side appear more distant as they are given less colour and detail.

Right: There is a strong impression of space in this landscape by Christopher Baker. The foreground is quite detailed and contains warm golds and greens, which come forward, but as we move back to the horizon the colours become progressively paler, cooler and lighter and the outlines of the trees less distinct.

These quick sketches by Ronald Jesty demonstrate the use of both linear and atmospheric perspective in giving depth and interest to a landscape scene. The subject is an avenue of trees on a fine but misty winter morning. The bare branches and twigs form net-like structures through which more distant trees can be seen, each plane becoming bluer and hazier as it recedes into the thin fog.

Had the artist chosen to place the avenue centrally, with the road running down the middle of the picture, he would have achieved a sense of depth but the composition would have been over-symmetrical and not very exciting. Instead, he sat down on the grass verge, facing the road at an angle. This vantage point creates a much more dynamic composition; the sharp diagonal of the road propels us inexorably into the picture, and the low "worm's-eye" view accentuates the diminishing scale of the trees as they move back in the picture.

Having sketched out the main elements of the composition in charcoal pencil (**above left**), the artist then established the tonal structure of the scene (**below left**). The shading depicts the varying amount of atmosphere between the viewer and the distant trees – the hazier and paler the forms, the further away they seem and this automatically creates a sense of distance.

In the watercolour sketch (**above**) we see how the artist treats foreground, middle ground and background almost as a series of "stage flats", with each plane fading progressively into the distance. The dark tone of the tree trunk in the right foreground is particularly important; not only does it provide a "frame" which concentrates our attention on the scene beyond, its strength of tone and detail also separates it from the planes behind, enhancing the illusion of three dimensions.

Generally, it is advisable to paint the hazier background of your picture first, gradually strengthening tones and colours as you progess toward the foreground. This applies particularly to watercolour, which is a medium requiring that you always paint from light to dark. Allow each layer of colour to dry completely before painting the next one, except in the background, where colours can be blurred together while still wet to create a misty effect.

CHOOSING YOUR VIEWPOINT

Before you begin a landscape painting, it is worth taking time to observe your subject from different angles and make several sketches of it. You will be surprised how even small changes of viewpoint can dramatically alter the perspective and the impression of depth in the scene.

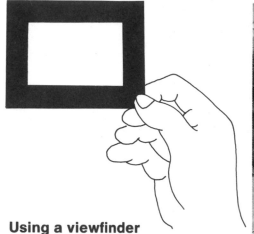

Using a viewfinder

A good landscape composition is one that conveys a feeling of depth, and in which the main elements of the picture combine to create a balanced and unified whole. When you look at a complex subject like a landscape, it can be difficult to decide on the best viewpoint from which to base your composition, and this is where a cardboard viewfinder comes in useful. It helps to train your eye to see and compose successful pictures. The edges of the viewfinder act as a "window frame" which isolates one section of the scene from the overall view so you can see it more clearly in terms of composition. Close one eye and look at your subject through the viewfinder, moving it this way and that, toward and away from you until the subject is framed in a pleasing way.

To make a viewfinder you will need a sheet of card, a steel ruler, a craft knife and a pencil. Draw a rectangle in the centre of the sheet of card, about 152mm × 102mm (6in × 4in). Cut out the window using the craft knife, and your viewfinder is ready for use.

Bird's eye view

We are used to looking at our surroundings from normal eye level, so seeing things from a high viewpoint is fascinating because it is relatively unfamiliar. Bear this in mind when you are painting landscapes and street scenes: an imaginative viewpoint can make for a more striking image. Climb up to the top of a hill and sketch the fields rolled out before you, or look out of an upper window to capture the unusual perspective of buildings, cars and figures in the street below.

Worm's eye view

Looking at a scene from a low viewpoint – or "worm's eye" view – also offers a fresh perspective on the landscape. If you position yourself at the bottom of a slope, for instance, a building at the top of the slope will tower dramatically above the horizon line. Similarly a low viewpoint will make foreground objects appear much larger than objects in the background, thus giving a dramatic sense of depth to the picture.

Indicating scale

By including a prominent foreground in the composition of a landscape you automatically provide an illusion of depth. The viewer instinctively compares the size of the foreground object with the size of features further away, particularly if the object is of known size, such as a tree or a figure. Alternatively, crouch down low to include a small foreground detail such as flowers or a rock. This immediately introduces an exciting element of scale into the view, as the foreground details will appear disproportionately large compared to elements in the distance.

Above: The scale of a landscape may be conveyed by your choice of viewpoint. Roy Herrick chose this dizzying vantage point because it best expresses the character of this particular location.

Right: Viewed in sharp perspective and from a low viewpoint, the impressive scale and grandeur of this classic building is given dramatic emphasis in this watercolour painting by Charlotte Halliday.

Lead-in lines

Use a foreground object to lead the eye toward the main focus of the painting, thus providing continuity between foreground and background. For example, position yourself so that a fence, river or pathway curves toward the background: this leads the eye into the composition, giving an impression of moving forward.

Charlotte Halliday 1984

PAINTING WATER

Water has always been a favourite painting subject. What artist can resist the challenge of portraying a sparkling stream, surf crashing against rocks, or the mirror-like surface of a calm, clear lake? Here, once again, an understanding of perspective will improve your seascapes and waterscapes enormously.

Above left: Using simple, almost abstract shapes, Michael Fairclough evokes the immensity of sea and sky. The upward sweep of the clouds offsets the horizontal lines of the waves and gives the composition freshness and movement.

Above right: The artist captures the smooth, silky surface of shallow water reflecting the setting sun: you can almost hear the waves sighing gently. The more simply you paint water, the more "watery" it looks. Rather than paint every ripple, it is better to paint two or three and let these represent the rest — the viewer will still see the picture as if they were all there.

Left: In this seascape by Alfred Sisley, note how the artist uses thick paint and vigorous strokes in the foreground only. The smooth brushwork of the distant sea indicates the foreshortening of the waves.

An obvious point, often overlooked, is that the laws of perspective apply in painting and drawing water just as they do for buildings, roads, fields and other landscape elements. Receding lines, and the diminishing scale of objects as they move further away, follow the same rules.

A common problem for beginners is that of making a stretch of water "lie down" and appear flat and horizontal as it recedes into the distance. If the perspective is wrong, it can appear as if the water is flowing uphill! There are several reasons why this might occur. Most often, it is because the vanishing point of the river, stream or whatever is positioned *above* the horizon line in the picture; consequently the water does not lie down but appears to slope upwards. Always check that a stretch of water in your picture stays on or below the horizon line.

Drawing bends in a river also presents problems of perspective. As the river curves out

of view, its shape becomes very much flatter and narrower, but if the angle of the bend is drawn too wide, again the river appears to slope upward. This is often due to lack of observation; the inexperienced artist draws what he knows and not what he sees.

Wave perspective
Another point to watch out for is the perspective of waves and ripples as they recede into the distance. When you are looking out to sea, for example, you will notice that the waves become foreshortened – they appear smaller and closer together as they approach the horizon. They also appear to flatten out. To convey this in your picture, paint only the foreground waves and ripples in detail, and use smaller strokes as you work back to the horizon. Paint the distant water with flat, horizontal strokes, with less detail and less tonal variation, until, at the horizon, the water is represented with flat washes of colour.

Above: This oil painting by William Garfit captures the languid atmosphere of the English countryside on a summer day. By starting the C-curve of the river on the bottom right, he coaxes the eye into the middle ground, where the gentle curve of the river invites you to linger a little longer in the picture. The river lies flat in the landscape because its shape is flatter and narrower as it recedes, and because the vanishing point is below the horizon.

REFLECTIONS IN WATER

Portraying reflections in water is not always as straightforward as it might seem, because the light and the movement of the water can play all kinds of visual tricks. However, if we remember that reflections obey certain laws of perspective, our task is made much easier. By making sketches of reflections in water and observing some simple rules, it won't be long before you can paint reflections effectively and with ease.

Right: The perspective lines of reflected objects converge toward the same vanishing point as the object itself.

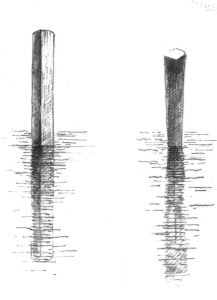

Left: An object leaning toward you creates a reflection that is longer than its foreshortened self.

Right: An object leaning away from you creates a reflection that is shorter than itself.

Above: In still water reflections are an exact mirror image of the reflected object. An object that stands upright in water produces a reflection of the same length.

Right: Here the gentle undulations of the water's surface cause the reflections of the jetty to lengthen and distort, creating interesting patterns in the foreground. David Curtis painted the reflections with rapid lines and "squiggles" which capture a sense of light and movement on the water. It takes a certain amount of nerve to work this freely, but the result is lively and captures the spirit of the subject.

Above: Careful observation of the reflections of horses, figures and rocks enhances the marvellous sense of atmosphere this painting generates. Because of the misty light, and because wet sand is less reflective than clear water, the reflections are pale and soft.

Above: In moving water, reflections break up and appear longer than the object reflected. In fact, sometimes the reflection may appear many times longer than the height of the reflected object.

Above right: Reflections broken by the ripples in the water are subject to the laws of linear perspective. The closer the ripples are to you, the larger and more widely spaced they are. As they recede, they appear smaller and closer together until, at the base of the object they become a dense mass.

Right: In this oil painting, Trevor Chamberlain has caught the atmosphere of a mellow autumn morning, with the calm, still water reflecting objects almost like a mirror. To capture the smooth surface of the water, the artist uses layers of thin, fluid paint and broad, soft strokes, subtly blending the edges of the reflections into the surrounding water.

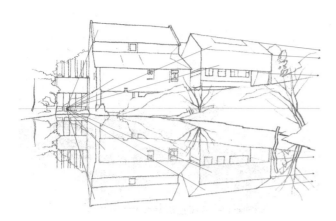

Ronald Jesty has made many sketches and paintings of this mill pond near his home, returning at different seasons and under different weather conditions to study the effects of light and movement on the water. He sits at the edge of the pond, almost at water level, so that his eye level is three or four feet above the surface. This position offers him a view of the buildings in the distance, as well as a close-up view of the water as it ripples away from the mill toward him.

The artist first makes an outline sketch of the scene (**above left**) in charcoal pencil. The perspective of the buildings and their reflected images is quite complex, and it is important to get the groundwork right before proceeding with a more finished working drawing in pencil (**above**). The painting (**below**) of the pond in winter was made in the studio and based on the working sketch.

Left: Another watercolour study, this time painted in high summer and executed on the spot using pan colours. Essentially, this is a study of the shapes and patterns of the ripples and reflections in the water as they come toward the artist. Notice the simplicity and economy with which the scene is painted: the essence of nature is often well described by a few convincing marks that remain fresh, where a confusion of paintwork and colours may fail.

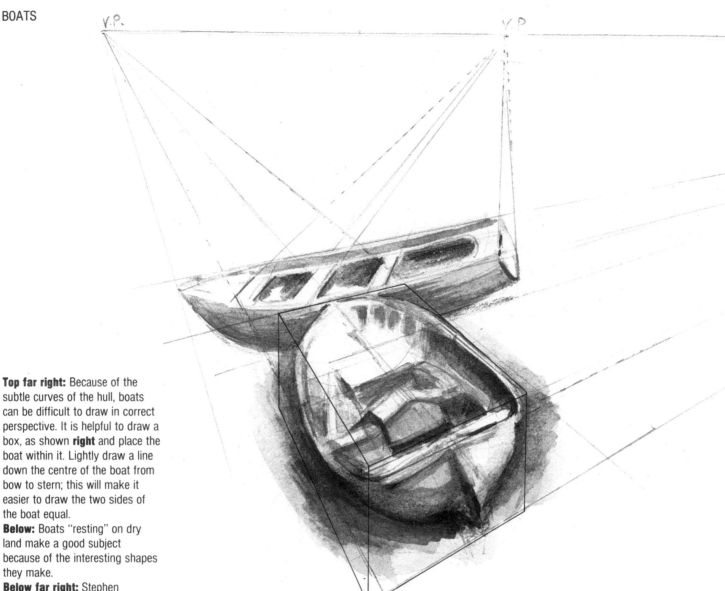

Top far right: Because of the subtle curves of the hull, boats can be difficult to draw in correct perspective. It is helpful to draw a box, as shown **right** and place the boat within it. Lightly draw a line down the centre of the boat from bow to stern; this will make it easier to draw the two sides of the boat equal.

Below: Boats "resting" on dry land make a good subject because of the interesting shapes they make.

Below far right: Stephen Crowther chose a low viewpoint and an oblique angle of perspective to exploit the ship's impressive dimensions.

Drawing boats

If you have tried to paint seascapes and harbour scenes, no doubt you have grappled with the problem of drawing boats in perspective. They are notoriously difficult to get right, and really the only answer is to keep practising drawing them. If you use the techniques for measuring and comparing described on pages 100–101 as a guide, and constantly analyze shapes and angles as you draw, then, in time, the accuracy of your drawing will improve enormously. For example, work out how many times the length of the hull divides into the height of the mast, if there is one. The curves of the boat's hull must be drawn accurately, and you must also get the width of the hull correct in relation to its length. A useful tip is to draw a box in perspective, as shown, **above**, and then draw the shape of the boat within that framework.

PERSPECTIVE IN SKIES

The sky is probably the most elusive subject for an artist to capture on
canvas or paper, yet because it determines the overall mood of a picture it is
an important part of the composition of any landscape.

Drawing and painting skies presents a special challenge. You have to cope with fickle weather, changing light and a subject that moves and alters shape before your very eyes. In addition, you have to try and convey the illusion of clouds and sky stretching away into infinity.

Conveying the illusion of recession in the sky means observing and recording the effects of atmospheric perspective, just as you would with the landscape. Think of the sky, not as a vertical backdrop to the landscape, but as a huge dome stretching across to the horizon. The sky is clearer directly overhead than at the horizon because we see it through less atmosphere. Toward the horizon, atmospheric haze gradually dims the landscape and sky with a thin veil. This is why clouds appear cooler and greyer in colour as they recede from our view.

The rules of diminishing perspective also apply, with the clouds nearest to you appearing larger and more clearly defined than those further away. As they recede toward the horizon, clouds overlap each other and appear smaller, flatter and closer together.

By varying the consistency of the paint and the type of brushstrokes used, you can create a range of subtle effects that suggest the amorphous nature of clouds and sky. Creamy, opaque colour will suggest groups of dense, advancing clouds; thinly applied, transparent colour gives the impression of atmosphere and recession, and is ideal for portraying retreating clouds and areas of dark, remote sky. To achieve the effect of distant haze, blend wet colour into wet, taking some of the sky colour into the land and vice versa. This slight obscuration of the horizon gives a marvellous sense of air and light.

Above: Here a few fluffy clouds laze across a summer sky. Leaving the cloud shapes as bare paper, Dennis Roxby-Bott applied a very thin wash of ultramarine blue for the sky, painting rapidly around the clouds so as to leave ragged edges. Pale washes of grey suggest the shadowed parts of the clouds.

Left: The sky can give power and atmosphere to the simplest landscape. Here Peter Burman uses atmospheric perspective to evoke the drama of dark storm clouds glowering over the Norfolk coast. The large foreground clouds are painted with vigorous strokes, making them project forward, while the clouds in the distance lose definition and blend into the horizon.

Below: David Carpanini used charcoal on white paper for this bleak, slightly eery impression of a Welsh mining village at dawn. The swirling, vortex-like rhythm of the clouds, echoed in the contours of the hills, leads the eye to the centre of interest — the huge metal structure silhouetted against the rising sun.

Clear skies

It is tempting to overstate the blue of the sky and make it too bright and too uniform in colour, so that instead of receding into space it comes forward like a wall. The most useful blues for skies are ultramarine, cobalt and cerulean, but in their pure state they are much too intense and must be subdued with other colours. Touches of alizarin crimson mixed with yellow ochre usually create the right balance for a clear sky, as do burnt umber, raw sienna and vermilion, plus white, of course, if you are using an opaque medium.

If you look closely at the sky you will see that it contains many subtle variations in colour and tone. Due to the effects of atmospheric haze, a blue sky appears brightest and warmest in colour directly overhead and pales toward the horizon, sometimes becoming yellowish or greenish. To suggest recession in a clear sky, introduce a note of warmth in the area near the top of the picture by using ultramarine (a rich, warm blue) perhaps mixed with a touch of alizarin crimson or violet. As you work down, begin to use cooler blues such as cobalt and cerulean, subdued with touches of other colours, as mentioned above. Near the horizon, there may be no blue at all but only pearly greys or pale yellows. While the paint is still wet, blend each "band" of colour into the next so that they merge imperceptibly into one another.

Top: A blue sky is often not as blue as we think. Here Dennis Roxby-Bott has painted the sky with a graduated wash of blue which pales into nothing as it nears the horizon. Watercolour, being transparent, is an excellent medium for painting skies. The luminosity of the white paper showing through a thin wash of colour helps the feeling of space, light and air.

Above: In watercolour, recession in a clear sky can be expressed effectively by means of a graduated wash. First dampen the area to be painted with clean water. Start with barely diluted colour at the top and steadily progress down the paper, decreasing the tone by adding more water to the pigment, until it becomes so pale it merges into the white paper.

Modelling clouds

John Ruskin's description of clouds as "sculptured mist" was very apt because, although they are soft and vaporous, clouds are also three-dimensional and have distinct planes of light and shadow. Clouds need careful handling as too heavy an application of paint can result in a dense, rock-like mass that is not suggestive of the airiness of the sky. The answer is to use thin, transparent layers of paint to retain the luminosity of the clouds, and to use warm and cool colours to model their forms. Warm colours — reds, oranges and yellows — advance, because our eyes are more receptive to them. Cool colours — blues, greens, violets and greys — recede. Therefore the contrast of warm and cool colours can be used to model the advancing and receding planes of clouds. The lit areas of cumulus clouds, for example, contain warm colours reflected from the sun — add subtle hints of yellow and pink to your whites in these areas. The other side of the cloud, in shadow, may be reflecting blue sky, so will appear a blue-grey.

Too many hard outlines make clouds appear "pasted on" to the sky and destroy the illusion of form. Partially blend the shadow edges of clouds into the sky so that they blend naturally into the surrounding atmosphere, with just a few crisp contours defining the furrows and ridges within the clouds. This contrast of hard and soft edges emphasizes form and adds interest, but remember that the contrast should be less pronounced as the clouds recede.

Top: Coastal skies often have a pearly quality of light, which Trevor Chamberlain captures in his painting of sailing boats. The warm blue of the sky overhead gives way to pale, creamy colours in the middle distance, and finally, near the horizon, to a misty grey. The nearest clouds are painted with a loose mixture of white and yellow ochre, scumbled lightly over the blue underlayer.

Above: The sky is transparent, but oil paint is opaque. To achieve an illusion of transparency, a good tip is to use loose, directional strokes instead of applying a flat, uniform layer of colour. Breaking up the paint surface in this way gives an impression of shimmering, vibrating light, particularly when small dabs of paint of different colour — but identical tone — are side by side.

Above: Instead of painting the sky as a flat area, John Martin uses broken colours laid over a warm-toned ground. This gives a more vivid impression of the sparkle of a summer sky.

Below: Here Stephen Darbyshire contrasts the fluffy shapes of the clouds with the hard-edged, geometric shapes of the buildings.

Right: This watercolour by Lucy Willis gives an exhilarating impression of space and moving cloud. The diminutive skaters on the ice emphasize the scale of the sky and landscape. To create the wintry sky, the colours were applied onto wet paper and allowed to bleed together, with downward strokes hinting at rain.

PERSPECTIVE IN SKIES

In the two stages leading up to the finished painting (**opposite**) Ronald Jesty shows how to convey a powerful feeling of perspective and scale. The flat landscape allows an unrestricted view of the sky, from almost overhead to the distant horizon. The horizon is placed very low and so emphasizes the broad mass of clouds which scud overhead and draw us into the picture.

By making a series of charcoal sketches, the artist establishes the composition, perspective and tones. In the outline sketch (**right**) he plots the position of his centre of vision, and draws lines radiating outwards from that point. This helps to establish the shapes and the perspective of the clouds, which appear smaller and flatter as they converge toward the horizon.

In the tonal sketch in charcoal (**below**) the artist then models the main shapes and masses of cloud.

Because of the rounded form of the clouds the gradation from light to dark is subtle, but here the shapes and tones are simplified in order to establish a firm impression of their three-dimensional shapes and of the direction of the light. It's also important to convey the tonal relationship between the sky and the land, and here the trees are much darker in comparison to the darkest tones in the sky: these darker tones in the landscape make the sky appear light and airy by contrast.

The final painting is executed in watercolour. The artist begins with the horizon, and then builds up the tones of the sky and landscape with successive washes, working from light to dark. A strong sense of recession in the sky, and of the clouds racing towards us, is achieved by painting the nearer clouds larger and stronger in tone than those in the distance.

INCLINED PLANES

Landscapes often feature hills and valleys, the contours of which not only add movement and rhythm to a picture but also emphasize the forms of the land. In addition, a series of slopes or inclined planes that recede into the distance can give a dramatic impression of depth, since the eye follows their progression from the foreground back toward the horizon.

When painting a flat landscape it is a relatively simple matter to establish horizon line, vanishing points and so on. But when the land undulates, and roads, paths and fences climb hillsides and descend into valleys, the perspective problems are slightly more complex, because a number of different vanishing points are involved. However, once the basic principles are understood, drawing inclined planes will come as second nature to you.

The parallel lines of a road sloping uphill will meet above the horizon. The steeper the slope the higher the vanishing point will be. Where the road slopes downhill, lines will vanish at a point below the horizon, the steeper the descent the lower the vanishing point. In other words, three-point perspective applies, because there are vanishing points above and below eye level.

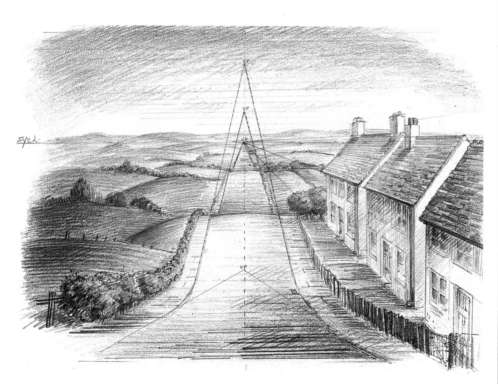

Above: Here the straight road slopes up and down as it disappears to the centre of vision at the horizon. The vanishing points for the inclines and declines are indicated. Though they stand on sloping ground, the houses are built on level foundations, therefore their vanishing point is on the horizon and not above it or below it. Note also the proportional narrowing of the fields as they recede towards the horizon.

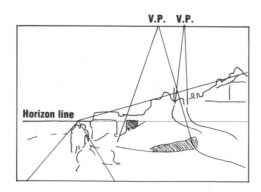

Below: Most landscapes will feature inclined planes, particularly if they include buildings with sloping roofs and gables. If correctly represented in perspective, inclined planes can add to the visual interest of a picture and give a feeling of recession. In Trevor Chamberlain's painting the sloping angles of the buildings and the grass bank break up the horizon in an interesting way.

TOWNSCAPES

Most people nowadays live in towns and cities, and buildings and streets make an immediately accessible subject for the study of shape, form, texture, pattern and perspective. Paintings and drawings of buildings can pose a number of exciting challenges and give you the opportunity to stretch your drawing and observational skills. An understanding of linear perspective is important, but you will also be applying atmospheric perspective, since buildings in the foreground appear stronger in tone and more clearly defined than those in the middle and far distance. This chapter shows you how to record accurately the basic structure of buildings and other man-made structures, and how to draw in perspective individual features such as arches, steps, rooftops and chimneys. In addition there is advice on selecting a viewpoint that will give a true impression of a structure's dimensions and perspective as well as its form and solidity.

The play of light and shadow on steps, arches and walls creates an almost abstract pattern of shapes in this acrylic painting by Jeremy Galton.

PERSPECTIVE IN BUILDINGS

A working knowledge of basic perspective is essential if your buildings and townscapes are to look solid and real, and a good way to start is by simplifying a building – breaking it down into geometric shapes such as cubes and cylinders and drawing the shapes in perspective. Having established the underlying structure of the building and its position in space, it is then comparatively easy to add the tonal and textural variations that give the building its unique but identifiable character.

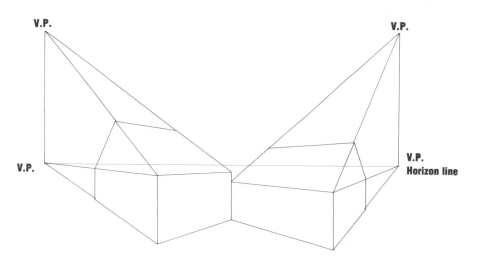

Above: Where the sides of buildings are visible, the horizontal lines of walls and roofs converge to vanishing points on the horizon while vertical lines meet at points overhead, directly in line with those beneath.

Above: Plotting the position of the apex of a pitched roof, when a building is viewed from the side, is a simple matter. Draw diagonal lines from the corners of the side wall: the point where they bisect is the centre. Take an upright from there after estimating the height of the roof. The apex of the roof should rest on the upright line.

Left: Be on the lookout for old or unusual buildings that have a bit of character. David Curtis positioned himself close to one corner of this old wooden boathouse so that he could include a view of the interior as well as the exterior of the building, with all its fascinating details.

Right: Stephen Crowther has risen to the challenge of painting a group of buildings facing in different directions and from a low viewpoint. A firm grasp of how three-point perspective works is necessary here.

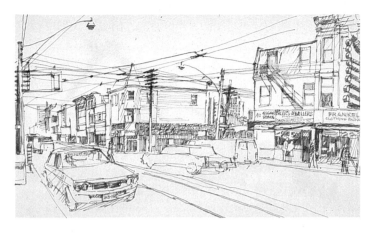

Simple structures

Buildings often appear complicated at first, because they are covered in all sorts of detail: chimneys, doors, windows, balconies and so on. However, underneath all that artifice, most architectural subjects are basically made up of a series of cubes – and if you can draw a cube in perspective you can certainly draw a building.

When drawing buildings, your viewpoint should be selected so that it not only shows the specific features and details but also creates a true impression of the building's dimensions and perspective. This can be done most effectively by choosing a position which enables two sides of the structure to be seen, usually

from one corner. This will create two vanishing points, which will help to create an impression of solidity and form far better than a "flat-on" view of the facade.

The method of drawing a building in two-point perspective is exactly the same as that for drawing a cube, described on pages 22–25. Begin with a simple sketch to establish the size and position of the building on your paper. The drawing doesn't have to be accurate at this stage: just plot the main outlines by eye. Now you can use perspective lines to check accuracy and make any necessary adjustments.

Note at what height the horizon line comes in relation to the building and draw it in lightly.

Above left and right: With a simple ballpoint pen and a sketchbook, you can make rapid, "on the spot" sketches.

Now extend the horizontal parallel lines of the building to the horizon line. The top and bottom lines of the building should meet at the same point on the horizon – the vanishing point. The horizontal lines of doors and windows should also meet at the same vanishing point.

If a building has projecting features such as an extension, balcony or porch, simply think of them as smaller boxes attached to the larger box. The same principles of perspective apply.

TRICKY PERSPECTIVE

Artists are drawn toward old buildings and structures because they have so much to offer in the way of interesting detail. Stairways, porticos, arches, towers and steeples all give a building its individual character, but drawing these features in correct perspective can be a headache. The answer lies in first reducing the structures to their basic geometric shapes and then drawing in the lines of perspective.

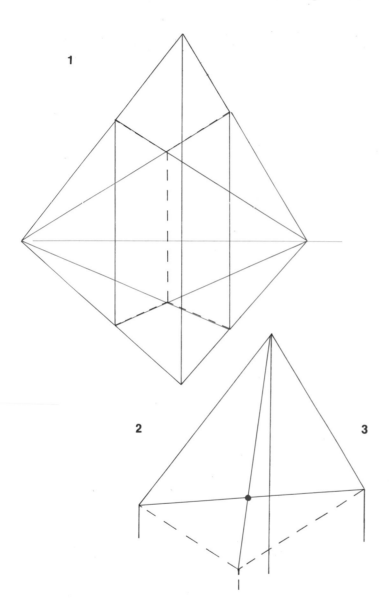

1

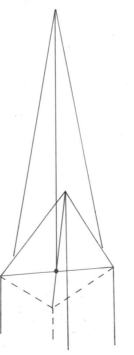

2

3

Church spires

One subject that people often find difficult is that of a church spire viewed from ground level. The problem is how to place the centre of the spire in correct relationship to the tower that supports it (the same problem arises with chimney pots resting on chimney stacks). The trick is to pinpoint the centre of the tower and align the centre of the spire with it, as shown **below**.

Steps and stairs

The perspective of steps and stairs is essentially the same as that of inclined and declined planes (see page 60). A staircase is basically wedge-shaped, so the vertical vanishing point can be located above or below the vanishing point of the base of the steps, depending on whether the steps are ascending or descending. The horizontal steps themselves, when viewed at an angle, converge to a point on the horizon line directly in line with your centre of vision.

4

Church spire

1 Draw the base of the church tower in 2-point perspective (refer to the instructions on page 24 if necessary).

2 Pinpoint the centre of the roof of the tower by drawing diagonal lines from the corners (**red**).

3 Estimate the height of the spire and draw a vertical line from the centre of the roof to its tip. Then draw the sloping sides of the spire.

4 With the spire in correct position, erase all working lines and complete the drawing.

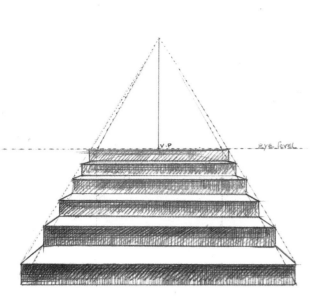

Above: A flight of steps viewed from the front will converge to a single vanishing point above the horizon line.

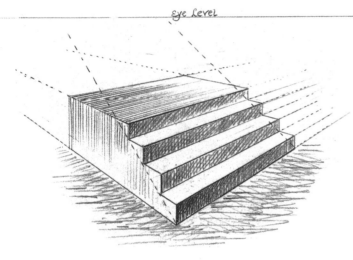

Above: A staircase seen at an angle is viewed in three-point perspective. There are two vanishing points on the horizon line and one above.

Above: We view steps in very sharp perspective when we are about to go down them. Note the narrowing of the steps as they descend from view.

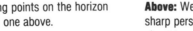

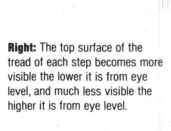

Right: The top surface of the tread of each step becomes more visible the lower it is from eye level, and much less visible the higher it is from eye level.

DRAWING BRIDGES

Old stone bridges have a charm of their own and offer the artist an opportunity to exploit contrasts of shape, tone and colour as well as interesting textures.

Drawing the arches of a bridge that is parallel to the picture plane is fairly simple. First, establish the horizon line and mark on it the vanishing point – which is directly opposite your eye if you are facing the bridge square-on. Then draw the outline of the bridge and its arches. Draw radiating lines extending from the vanishing point to the bottom corner of each arch to establish the perspective of the inner walls of the arches.

A bridge facing at an angle to the picture plane makes for a more interesting composition because lines that slope in from the edges of the picture give a greater feeling of depth. However, the elliptical curves of the receding arches must be placed correctly in perspective if the bridge is to look at all convincing. Don't despair: there is a simple method, as outlined on the opposite page. The same method can also be used for constructing any series of shapes of similar width that pan away in perspective, such as a row of house fronts or a line of evenly spaced telegraph poles.

Below: In this painting by Trevor Chamberlain, the bridge in the distance forms a link between the various elements of the composition. Through the arches we get a tantalizing glimpse of the river beyond.
Right: In John Newberry's painting the bridge forms a dramatic diagonal across the picture plane.

Arches in perspective

First plot the horizon line in position on your paper (blue). Having decided on the height of the first upright, draw the receding lines of the top and base of the bridge so that they meet at the vanishing point (black). Draw a horizontal line exactly halfway up the first upright, extending to the vanishing point (red). Draw in the second upright after estimating its distance from the first upright. Now take a diagonal line from the top of the first upright through the centre of the second (A1). Where it meets the base line, position your third upright. Similarly, take a line from the top of the second upright through the centre point of the third, and where it meets the base line you position your fourth upright (B2). Repeat until you reach the end of the bridge.

Below right: To draw the rounded top of an arch in perspective, first find the centre of the opening by plotting the diagonals — the centre is where they cross. Take an upright from there (red) and you have the top of the arch. Then draw arcs as shown. Notice that, due to perspective recession, the nearer half of the arch appears larger than the further half.

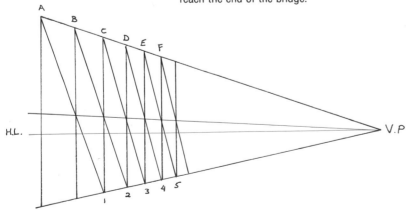

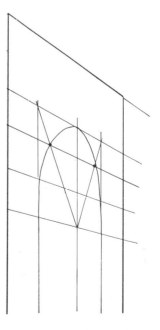

Left: In towns and cities, the precise shapes of buildings and other architectural features such as bridges afford the opportunity to create bold, geometrical compositions. Stephen Crowther painted this view of the river Arno in Florence from a window on a hill above the city.

Below left: On a sketchbook page an artist has recorded a panoramic view of the Grand Canal in Venice. The tiny figures on the steps are vital in establishing the scale of the scene. If you want to capture the spirit of a place, there is no better way than by making on-the-spot sketches like this. Photographs can be a useful reference, but they tend to destroy detail and perspective. Besides, while you are sketching you are unconsciously absorbing the sounds, the smells, the "flavour" of the place, and all of this will be reflected in your drawing.

Below: Pastels and coloured pencils are a handy sketching medium if you want to make colour notations.

Left: Painting a busy street scene on-the-spot is somewhat impractical, but you can usually slip into a doorway to make sketches and colour notes on which to base a painting done later in the studio. This has a distinct advantage because memory tends to "edit out" superfluous detail and you are left with a fresher, more direct impression of the scene.

For this painting, Ken Howard chose a vertical format to emphasize the tall buildings, and the sharp perspective contributes to the vivid impression of a narrow city street.

Right: There are several perspective challenges in this view of an unusual street corner in London, such as the angle of the building, the windowless wall with its pseudo-classical columns and arch, the slope of the attic roofs, the chimney stacks and the dormer windows, and so on.

The artist, Charlotte Halliday, is a keen observer of architectural detail, and this is very apparent in her sensitive pencil and watercolour painting. The angle of light on the various planes and the contrasts of light and shade on the different architectural elements are superbly executed. A composition of this complexity relies far more on the accurate observation of the artist, than on mastery of anything more than simple two-point perspective.

STILL LIFE AND INTERIORS

Our homes and immediate surroundings, because of their very familiarity, are often overlooked as suitable areas of inspiration, yet even the most mundane of everyday objects can make exciting compositions. There are obvious practical advantages in choosing to paint interiors and still lifes. You have none of the uncertainties of landscape painting, with its changing weather and light; you can control the lighting and group objects as you want them; and, of course, you can work in warmth and comfort! In this chapter you will discover ways of using perspective to define the scale and form of the objects in a still life or interior. The section on still life shows you how to compose a group of objects effectively, how to use light and shade to model forms, how to draw rounded shapes such as bottles and jugs in perspective, and how to paint plants and flowers. The section on interiors shows you how to draw a room and the objects within it in perspective, and how to achieve a sense of space and atmosphere within the room.

This watercolour painting by Keith Andrew explores the wonderful subtleties of light and tone that occur in interiors.

PAINTING STILL LIFE

Unlike landscapes and figure subjects, still life allows you to control the selection and arrangement of the objects you wish to paint. No matter how short of time you are, or how cramped the area in which you paint, a still life can be set up in minutes and will give you unlimited scope for the study of shape, form, space, light and colour.

When setting up a still life for the first time, don't be tempted to include too much. A simple arrangement of three or four objects, selected for their different qualities of shape, form and colour, will be quite sufficient. When you have made an arrangement that pleases you, move around the group and sketch it from different angles and eye levels to see which makes the better composition. There is plenty to think about: does the light cast interesting shadows and highlights that describe the forms? Is there sufficient contrast of tone, colour and texture? Is there a reasonable variety of curves, shapes and tonal contrasts? You might want to rearrange the objects in the group, or change your own position in relation to the group, and this you can do as often as you like, until you are satisfied with the overall balance of the composition.

Space and depth
Try to arrange your still life in a way that emphasizes the form and structure of the objects and the spaces between them. Space and depth in a still life can be depicted in a number of ways, as shown opposite.

Right: Place light shapes in front of dark shapes and dark ones in front of light. Strong contrasts of tone emphasize contours and separate one object from another, thus creating spatial depth.

Left: Make detail and texture sharper in the foreground. Render the edges softer and the forms less distinct further back, to make them recede.

Left below: Use brighter, warmer colours such as reds, oranges or yellows in the nearer objects to make them come forward, and softer, more neutral colours in the background objects to make them recede.

Left: Place objects so as to emphasize their form: a box, for example, looks more three-dimensional when we can see two or more of its planes; a jug looks more round when we can see inside the rim.

DEFINING FORM

How do you set about describing solid, three-dimensional forms on a flat piece of paper or canvas? The answer lies in using tone – degrees of light and dark – to show both the direction of light and the changes of plane on objects.

All solid forms are made up of planes, and the way light strikes these planes helps to reveal the volume and solidity of objects. The main way in which form can be suggested in a drawing or painting is by using light, middle and dark tones to define the light and dark areas of the subject. Your eyes interpret this information as showing which parts of the object are nearest to the source of light and which ones are further away. The exact place where light changes to dark tells you whether the object is curved or angular.

To understand how lights, halftones and shadows work, take a sheet of white paper and hold it to the right of a lamp. Bend the paper into a slight curve and observe how the right side of the paper becomes slightly darker in tone. Now bend the paper further round, and you will see that the left side remains fully lit while the middle and right sections show a gradual transition from halftone to shadow which describes the smooth curve of the surface. Finally, fold the paper down the middle,

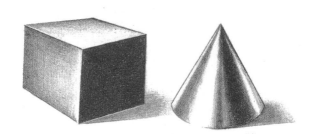
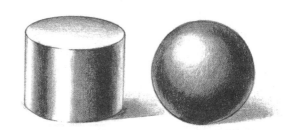

Left: These diagrams show the pattern of light and shadow that falls on a cube, a cone, a cylinder and a sphere. These four simple shapes are the main basic forms to be found in nature and can be used to simplify your understanding of any object you draw, no matter how complex.

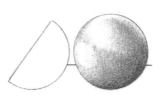

Right: Ronald Jesty achieves unity and variety in this composition by choosing objects whose shapes subtly echo each other. The play of light and shade on the spherical forms of the poppies, oranges and brandy bottle sets up a rhythmical pattern of circles, half-circles and ellipses, which gives a pleasing "wholeness" to the picture.

open it out, and notice the sharp division between light and shadow where the two planes meet at the corner.

When it comes to approaching more complicated subjects – fruits, flowers and so on in a still life, or figures, or buildings and trees in a landscape – it helps to visualize them first as simple geometric shapes. All the objects around us are combinations of the curves and planes found in the sphere, the cone, the cylinder and the cube. A bottle is basically a cylinder, fruits are mostly spherical or near-spherical in shape, a table on which you may have arranged a still life group is basically a cube, and so on. Once you understand how to model these simple forms with light and shade, you will find it much easier to apply the same principles to objects with less easily defined forms, such as flowers and drapery.

The cube is the simplest form to draw as a solid object using light and shade since its flat

faces and straight edges can be drawn with relative ease and the planes have distinct and easily comparable tones. In rounded objects, however, the shading emerges slowly, with no sudden change from one tone to the next, and the tones need to be carefully blended together to give a smooth gradation. At the point nearest to the light source you have the highlight. From here, the area of main, or direct light, gradually becomes darker as the curved plane of the object turns away from the light. One important point to note is that the darkest shadow tone falls not at the extreme, furthest edge from the light, but just inside that edge. Beyond the area of shadow there will be a thin sliver of lighter tone, caused by reflection. Light striking the surface on which an object rests, or a nearby surface, will bounce back onto the shadow side. This is known as reflected light, and is a valuable tip when trying to draw or paint full, rounded forms.

Above: Drawing a plain white jug against a plain white background is a good way to train your eye to evaluate the tonal gradations that describe an object's form. Here the shadows are built up gradually with lightly hatched strokes.
Top: In this still life by Jacqueline Rizvi, contours are defined away from the light but "lost" where they face the light, indicating the volume of the objects.

LIGHTING A STILL LIFE

When setting up a still life group, consider the lighting carefully. The way in which patterns of light and shadow move through the group helps to lead the eye through the composition and thus creates a feeling of depth and three-dimensional space. In addition, contrasts of light and shade suggest solidity and the illusion of form. It is best to keep the lighting simple, preferably from a single source.

Side light
When light falls on the subject directly from one side, dramatic contrasts of light and shade are created, and texture is accentuated. Side light also creates strong cast shadows, which create visual "pathways" that link objects together and help to unify the group.

Three-quarter light
When light falls on the subject from slightly above and to one side (an angle of about 45°) it creates a strong impression of form and volume as well as picking out details of surface texture.

Above: A still life doesn't have to be complicated — it can consist of a single item. In this watercolour study, Jacqueline Rizvi sets a simple porcelain bowl against an expanse of white cloth. Light coming from the right casts a strong shadow inside the bowl which aids in the illusion of three dimensions. The cast shadow on the cloth helps to anchor the bowl, giving a sense of space and weight.

Back lighting

Diffused light from behind the group creates a soft halo of light around the objects. While colour and detail are minimized, being mainly lost in shadow, the overall effect is delicate and atmospheric.

CIRCLES IN PERSPECTIVE

Perhaps the most difficult of all shapes to draw in perspective are circles and spheres. Any circular shape, when viewed from an oblique angle, flattens out and becomes an ellipse. Whenever you draw bottles, glasses, jugs, bowls, cups, domes, wheels, hats or other cylindrical, spherical or half-spherical objects, you are involved with the challenge of drawing ellipses.

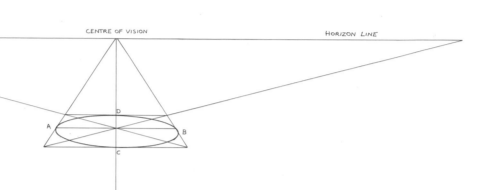

Above: To draw an accurate ellipse, first draw a square in perspective and draw in the diagonals to plot the centre. Draw a horizontal line through the centre from **A** to **B**. Now draw the front half of the circle freehand from **A** to **B**, touching **C**. Do the same with the back half of the circle, touching **D**.

Anyone can draw a straight line — you can always resort to using a ruler — but drawing circular objects in perspective requires a little more skill. A common problem is that of getting the two halves of an elliptical shape such as the rim of a cup to look equal — invariably our first attempts resemble lop-sided rejects from a beginners' pottery class! Yet there is a simple

method which will overcome this problem. Since the perfect circle fits into the perfect square, it follows that by drawing a square in perspective and fitting a circle into that square, we will obtain an accurate ellipse. The diagram above illustrates how an ellipse can be constructed using this method. Of course, this is a rather mechanical way of drawing, but it helps to

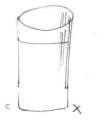

Above: Drawing ellipses takes practice. These sketches demonstrate two common errors, and how to correct them.

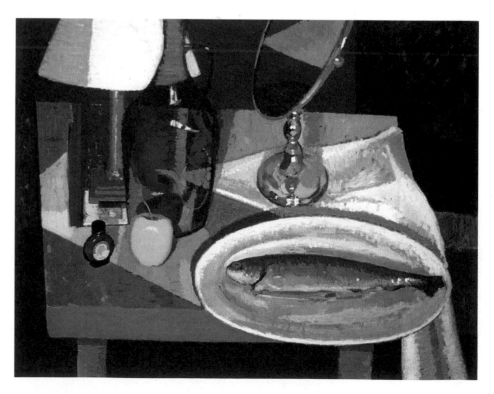

Above: Jacqueline Rizvi's painting of a cup and saucer shows how, when the eye level is high, the ellipse of the rim of the cup is very open. The rim of the saucer, being further from the eye than the cup, shows an even more open ellipse. Because the saucer is seen from a foreshortened viewpoint, the dip in which the cup rests appears to drop out of centre and come forward.

Left: In this beautifully structured composition by James Lee, elliptical shapes are played off against the diagonals of the table and cloth.

begin with. Frequent practice will give you the confidence to tackle ellipses freehand later on.

The rules governing the perspective of curved lines are in principle the same as for straight lines. Just as you see less and less of the top of a box the lower your eye level is, so you will see less and less of the opening of a cup or bowl as your eye lowers. In other words, an ellipse closes, or flattens out, the closer it gets to your eye level. The further away it gets, the more open it is. This point can be illustrated by drawing a clear glass bottle or a tall glass. If your eye level is above the object, the base is further from it than the rim, hence the curve of the base is more open than that of the rim.

The drawings on the opposite page illustrate two of the most common errors made when drawing spherical shapes. In **A** the ends of the ellipses formed by the rim and base of the glass are pointed. This is incorrect: an ellipse is

curved all the way around, as shown **B**.

In **C** the top of the glass has been drawn as if we were looking down on it, while the bottom of the glass is flat. Wrong again: the lower an ellipse drops away from the eye level, the more open becomes the curve, as shown **D**.

To practise drawing ellipses, make a sketch of a group of bottles, glasses and jars, all of varying heights. Establish your eye line lightly on the paper. You will notice how each ellipse varies in openness according to its distance from your eye level. Don't press hard with your pencil and try to draw the ellipse in one single line, but hold the pencil lightly and "feel out" the form as you draw. Use light, feathery strokes and go over your lines again if necessary until you are satisfied that the shape is correct. You can either erase those lines you don't need, or leave them in — the drawings will look more alive and energetic.

PLANTS AND FLOWERS

Flowers and plants are often included in still life groups, and you may like to present them as the main subject. Along with their qualities of grace, beauty and elegance, flowers appeal to all artists for their infinite variety of shape and colour. You can easily fill a sketchbook with endless studies and sketch notes on individual flowers, leaves, stems, buds and seedheads. It is a good idea to do this even if you are a complete beginner, as it will give you invaluable insight into botanical form and structure.

Arranging flowers

Flowers in a still life should look fresh and natural. Don't cram too many flowers into the vase: choose just a few, use an appropriate vase, then let them fall naturally, adjusting the blooms here and there so that you create different head levels and the flowers face in different directions, including profile views.

Flower shapes

Break down flower and leaf shapes into simple shapes then gradually add more detail and refine the outlines. Different flowers suggest different geometric shapes: wheels and circles are suggested by daisies, pansies and anemones; cups and cones are suggested by tulips and lilies, and so on.

Flower studies

Make detailed pencil drawings of flowers and plants in close-up. Careful observation helps you to understand the forms of petals, leaves and stems. Without this knowledge your paintings will be unconvincing.

Lost and found edges

When you paint a vase of flowers, try to convey an impression of some flowers being further back than others. This is done by bringing the nearer flowers into sharp focus while playing down those further back in the group. Pick out one or two flowers near the front and emphasize these with crisp, "found" edges. Make the flowers further back less well defined by using soft, "lost" edges and more muted colours. If every flower is given equal emphasis, the feeling of depth is lost.

Left: Here Trevor Chamberlain uses loose, fluid strokes to blend the edges of the petals and leaves into the surrounding atmosphere.
Right: Unexpected elements — in this case a mirror — can make a floral still life fresh and exciting. Here the mirror reflects part of the group, creating the illusion of greater space and depth.

Right: An informal grouping of daisies and blue clematis. The flowers at the front are given more definition than those behind and some flowers touch and overlap, thus creating the illusion of three dimensions.

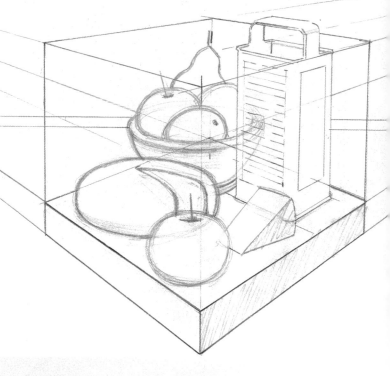

Composing a still life

The best way to learn how to portray the three-dimensional form of objects in colour is to try painting some simple objects from the kitchen.

This small collection of round and angular shapes makes an ideal subject for the study of perspective and modelling. In the drawing **right**, the objects have been simplified to their basic geometric shapes. We can see that the group as a whole fits into a "cube" viewed in two-point perspective, with the chopping board forming the base of the cube.

The first washes of colour are applied **below**, starting with the palest tones. Note how the whole of the fruit bowl has been drawn in, even though it is partially

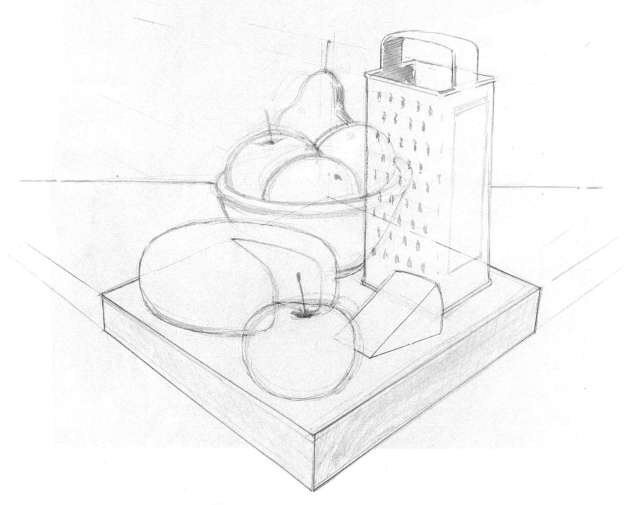

hidden by the cheese grater; this makes it easier to get the smooth rhythm of its elliptical shape.

The darks and mid tones are built up with thin layers of colour **below**. The artist develops the forms by darkening and refining the shapes of the shadows and the cast shadows, which anchor the objects to the surface of the table. The background is painted with loose, scrubby strokes which relieve the monotony of a flat area without being too "busy".

PERSPECTIVE IN INTERIORS

Perspective in interiors works in the same way as it does out of doors, and drawing an interior is challenging: not only do you have to get the perspective of the room right, because any errors will be immediately obvious, you also have to draw objects within the room in perspective and to the correct scale.

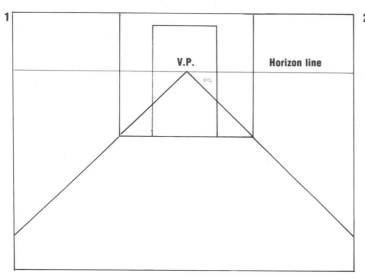

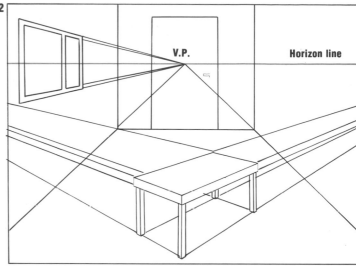

Perspective of a room

1 Draw the vertical and horizontal lines of walls and doors facing you. Draw the receding lines of the side walls. They should meet at your centre of vision on the eye level.

2 The horizontal lines of windows and doors will converge to the vanishing point. Objects at an angle to the picture plane will have two sets of converging lines on the same eye level.

Left: A small corner of a room presents an interesting compositional challenge. Here, the shadowy tones of the interior are dramatically broken by a shaft of sunlight slanting through the window onto the floor.

Right: Lucy Willis positioned herself at a turning in the stairs to paint this scene. The rhythm of curves and lines adds up to an exhilarating and highly unusual composition.

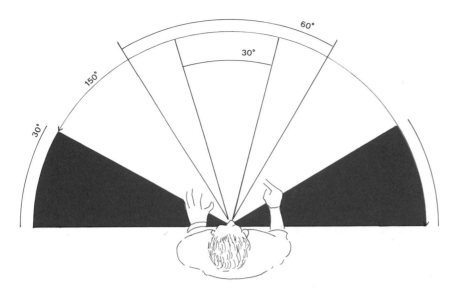

Cone of vision

Our normal field of clear vision ranges between 30 and 60 degrees. This narrow field of clear vision is known as the cone of vision. When drawing interiors — or indeed any subject — try not to include more than what is encompassed within your cone of vision. Taking in a "wide angle" view leads to distortions in perspective. Although this is perfectly acceptable, and produces interesting pictures, it is best to avoid it in the early stages, until you have fully grasped the rules of perspective and feel confident enough to break them.

Although most drawings and paintings of interiors depict only part of a room, it is as well to learn the basic principles for drawing a whole room, as this will enable you to work out angles of perspective more accurately when you come to paint a real interior.

To simplify the process of drawing a room in perspective, think of it as being the inside of a box. Standing in the middle of the "box", begin by drawing the horizontal and vertical lines of the far wall. Then establish the position of the horizon line, or eye level, by looking directly ahead and holding your pencil at arm's length, horizontally, in front of your eyes. Lightly draw the horizon line at the relevant point on your paper and mark, with a small circle, the spot where your point of vision falls. This is the vanishing point. Now you will be able to work out how the parallel lines of floor, ceiling, doors and windows, if continued, appear to converge at this vanishing point.

Now try the same exercise, only this time take up a position over to one side of the room. Once again, all the parallel lines will converge at your point of vision. Having established the vanishing point, you can now draw in the windows, doors, pictures, and any other objects that are parallel with the walls.

When an object such as a table is set at an angle to the picture plane, two-point perspective comes into play. There are now two sets of converging lines and two vanishing points, which are likely to extend beyond the limits of the paper.

Often the corner of a room makes a good starting point for a study of perspective. Once again the principle is quite simple: because there are two walls, there will be two sets of converging lines and two vanishing points.

OBJECTS IN INTERIORS

Interiors are full of objects, from large pieces of furniture to small pictures and ornaments. Try to spend some time drawing individual items – a chair, the folds in a curtain, an open window. This will help you draw them in perspective and to understand their underlying structure.

Below: A favourite room is a good place to begin your study of interiors and the objects within them. To paint this atmospheric, period room, Lucy Willis positioned herself opposite one corner. This creates a "wide angle" view which emphasizes the magnificent proportions of the room.

Above: Look for unusual viewpoints that offer a different perspective on a familiar scene. Here Lucy Willis looks down into the room from a gallery above; this "bird's eye" view of the tables laden with bowls and jugs creates an eye-catching composition.

Left: Chairs and other items of furniture can be drawn more accurately and more confidently if you first reduce them to their basic geometric forms. Imagine the legs and seat of a chair, for instance, as comprising a cube; the legs form the four corners of the cube's base, and the seat the top. It is then easier to represent the basic structure of the chair in correct perspective.

Often in interiors, you will be drawing objects that are placed at odd angles to the picture plane. Tables and chairs, for example, are often seen from a high viewpoint and it is all too easy to make the legs look lopsided or floating above the floor.

Don't panic, just imagine and then sketch the objects as simple geometric forms. In a drawing of a chair, for example, the points connecting the seat, the legs and the floor form a cube whose parallel lines converge at an imaginary vanishing point behind the chair. The next stage is to imagine that the chair is made of glass, and that you can see through to the back legs of the chair. Draw the back legs as if you can see them, even though in reality you can't. Experiencing the three-dimensional form of an object enables you to draw it more convincingly.

CREATING ATMOSPHERE

When painting outdoors, we can clearly see the way in which shapes, colours and tones become less and less distinct as they recede towards the horizon. Inside a room, the visual space between foreground and background is much narrower than in a landscape, so the effects of atmospheric perspective are much less obvious.

Faced with the problem of depicting a room in three dimensions on a two-dimensional surface, we still have to use optical devices to create an illusion of three dimensions. We can place objects in space by drawing them in perspective, but to reinforce the feeling of depth it is necessary to make use of tonal perspective. Strong lines and dark tones appear to be nearest to the viewer, so use these in the foreground and contrast them with lighter tones and softer lines in the background, indicating that they are further back in space or enveloped in shadow. This not only creates a sense of space, it also mimics the way our eyes perceive things: we can only focus on one small area at a time, and everything around that point is seen slightly out of focus.

Right: Here Jane Corsellis has used thin glazes and scumbles of oil colour which allow the warm-toned ground to show through in places. The broken nature of the paint and the partial mixing of colours brings a sense of vibrating light and air to this interior scene.

During the first decade of the 20th century the Danish painter Vilhelm Hammershoi painted many pictures of the interior of his historic Copenhagen residence, in which the dominant theme was the play of light in the sombre recesses of its rooms. In his *Woman Sewing in an Interior* **above**, space is defined by the white light that pours through the window and glows softly off the surfaces and planes of the room. The haunted emptiness of the room, the woman mutely absorbed in her work, and the spare, almost monochromatic colouring of the painting all give a sensation of a moment frozen in time.

A ROOM WITH A VIEW

An interior scene takes on a whole new dimension when you include the additional space that can be seen through a window or an open door. By depicting a part of the inside of the room as well as what can be seen outside it, you create an intriguing double image – a frame within a frame. The inclusion of a distant view seen through a door or window also opens up the picture space and increases the feeling of space and recession, drawing the viewer deeper into the picture.

Left: Here the geometry of verticals and horizontals formed by the walls and doorway is offset by the soft washes of watercolour that give an impression of light from outside penetrating the interior and reflecting off the surfaces of walls and floor.

Far left: One of the interesting aspects of an inside-outside view is the contrasts of tone and colour that occur between the interior and the exterior. In this painting by Joanna Wills, the hot sun outside emphasizes the coolness of the enclosed space of the room. The use of complementary colours – blue and yellow – accentuates the high-key mood.

Left: To emphasize depth in a composition, include objects of known size in the foreground, as Lucy Willis has done here. Viewed close up, the jugs and bowls on the windowsill appear much bigger than the distant trees seen through the window, and this contrast in scale accentuates the impression of receding space outside.

Right: Jane Corsellis delights in painting the glow and vibrancy of sunlight filtering into a room from outside. In this painting the room features more prominently than the view, yet there is a strong sense of the outside world being brought indoors.

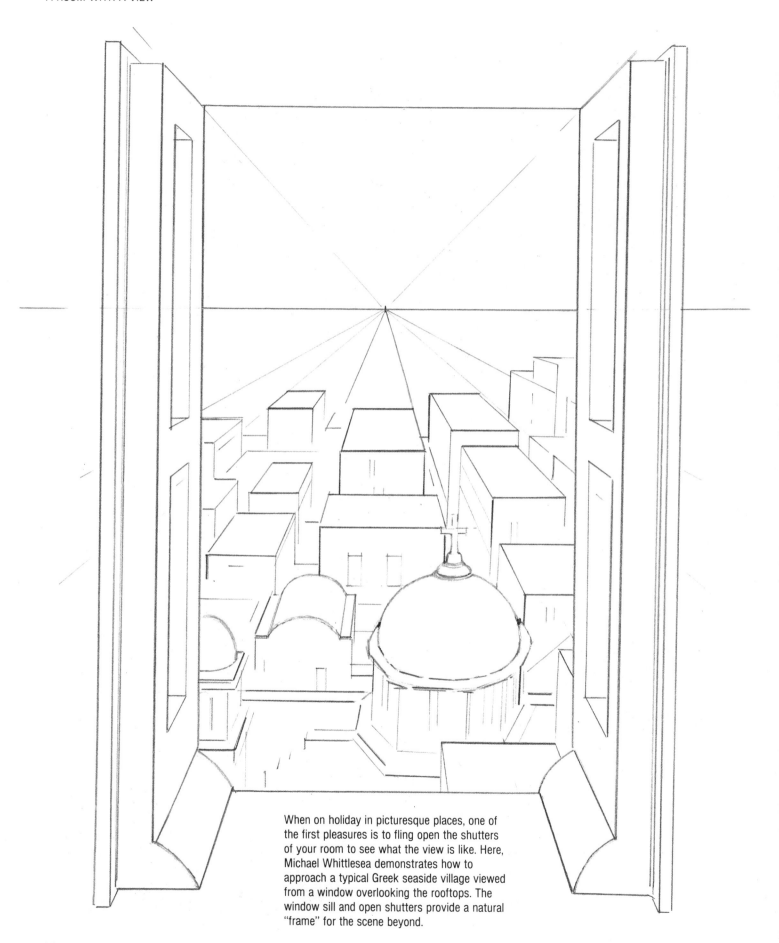

When on holiday in picturesque places, one of
the first pleasures is to fling open the shutters
of your room to see what the view is like. Here,
Michael Whittlesea demonstrates how to
approach a typical Greek seaside village viewed
from a window overlooking the rooftops. The
window sill and open shutters provide a natural
"frame" for the scene beyond.

Left: There is no difficulty in establishing the horizon line in this scene – it is, of course, the point where the sky meets the sea. It is then a simple matter to draw the buildings and the window shutters in perspective, with all parallel horizontal lines converging at the vanishing point directly ahead of the artist.

Above: After transferring the drawing onto watercolour paper, and with a little more detail added, the colour is then applied slowly and carefully, beginning with the lightest tones and colours and building up to the mid tones.

Right: The interior of the room is dark compared to the view outside; this frame of dark tone in the foreground intensifies the colours within the frame and also helps to separate foreground from background, creating a sense of depth and recession.

THE FIGURE

Of all the subjects which an artist is likely to tackle, the human figure is undoubtedly the most challenging. If you can learn to paint figures well then you will be able to paint anything competently. It is not essential to have a thorough knowledge of anatomy in order to draw figures successfully. What is needed, however, as with drawing any subject, is a keen and analytical eye, and a willingness to keep practising even if your first attempts are unsuccessful. Learning to interpret accurately the proportions of the body and at the same time instil a feeling of life into a figure is a real test of the artist's skill. One of the main problems encountered in drawing and painting the figure is the foreshortening that occurs in certain poses; constant measurement and reassessment will help to ensure that your drawing is accurate, and this chapter offers practical advice on how to measure scale and proportion.

A figure study in pen and ink by Lucy Willis, in which form and modelling are achieved by building up the tones with hatching and crosshatching.

MEASURING BY PENCIL

By using your pencil as a measuring tool for comparing the length of one part of your subject relative to the length of another part, you can keep a check on proportions as you draw, thus ensuring an accurate end result.

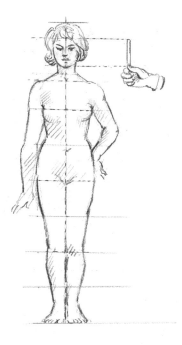

Choose a single dimension out of the subject — say the length of an arm — and use this as the key measure by which to gauge the proportions of all the other dimensions of the figure.

Grasping your pencil at its base, hold it at arm's length, elbow locked, in front of the subject. Keeping your head still, and with one eye closed, line up the tip of the pencil with, say, one end of the arm and mark the position of the other end with your thumbnail. Now you can compare the length of your key measure with other parts of the body. Keeping your thumbnail in the same position, and your arm still outstretched, move the pencil to another area of the figure, such as the upper leg, and compare its length with the length of your key measure. Make frequent comparative measurements like this throughout the drawing process to ensure that limbs, head and torso

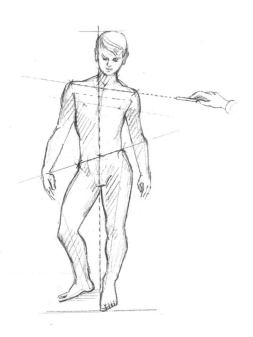

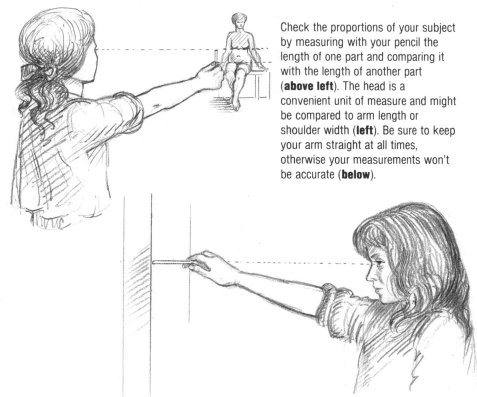

Check the proportions of your subject by measuring with your pencil the length of one part and comparing it with the length of another part (**above left**). The head is a convenient unit of measure and might be compared to arm length or shoulder width (**left**). Be sure to keep your arm straight at all times, otherwise your measurements won't be accurate (**below**).

are in proportion with each other.

A carpenter uses a spirit level and plumb line to check horizontals and verticals while he's building. While you're drawing, try using your pencil, like a carpenter's tool, to establish the vertical and horizontal alignments of your subject. This helps you not only to check scale and proportion but also to capture the essence of the model's pose. Simply extend your pencil in front of you over the subject as before, and turn it at various angles to line up one part of the model with another. Make a rough outline of the figure first and then use your measuring tool as a means of checking that you've got the horizontal and vertical alignments right.

A trap that is easy to fall into is to start a drawing of a figure at the top of the head and work down to the feet. This often leads to failure, for two reasons. First, unless you have a very good eye it is likely that some part of the figure will be out of proportion to the rest because you have lost sight of the relationship between one area of the figure and another. Second, you may well run out of space as you reach the bottom of the paper, so your unfortunate sitter ends up either with oddly shrunken legs or no feet at all!

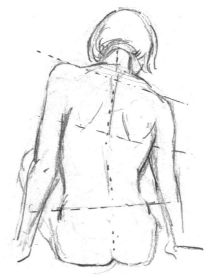

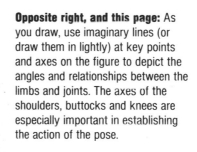

Opposite right, and this page: As you draw, use imaginary lines (or draw them in lightly) at key points and axes on the figure to depict the angles and relationships between the limbs and joints. The axes of the shoulders, buttocks and knees are especially important in establishing the action of the pose.

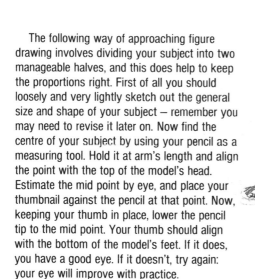

The following way of approaching figure drawing involves dividing your subject into two manageable halves, and this does help to keep the proportions right. First of all you should loosely and very lightly sketch out the general size and shape of your subject – remember you may need to revise it later on. Now find the centre of your subject by using your pencil as a measuring tool. Hold it at arm's length and align the point with the top of the model's head. Estimate the mid point by eye, and place your thumbnail against the pencil at that point. Now, keeping your thumb in place, lower the pencil tip to the mid point. Your thumb should align with the bottom of the model's feet. If it does, you have a good eye. If it doesn't, try again: your eye will improve with practice.

Having found the centre of your subject, mark its position at the centre of your outline drawing. This centre point gives you a means of checking the proportions of your figure as you draw. If your initial rough outline of the upper half extends below the mid point, or doesn't quite reach it, you will know that half of your drawing is either too large or too small, and can easily make any necessary adjustments.

Left: To set the figure on a solid base, it is often helpful to sketch in a platform on which the model can stand and to which the angles of the body can be related.

Right: The groups of figures in this composition, as the perspective lines indicate, can be set in space through the use of linear perspective. Measurements do not have to be exact, but to give an illusion of recession, vanishing points can be located and the figures placed accordingly in the correct scale.

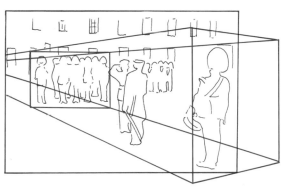

Left: In figure drawing, the rules of perspective must be employed to suggest depth, solidity and balance. The lines through the shoulders, hips and knees indicate the angle of the figure in relation to the picture plane.

FORESHORTENING

Foreshortening is a fascinating aspect of figure drawing, and it is worth getting to grips with because it allows you to tackle more interesting and imaginative poses.

In almost any pose, some parts of the body — limbs in particular — are likely to be foreshortened. That is, they project forward or recede backward and are thus subject to the laws of linear perspective. In an extremely foreshortened view — such as an end-on view of a reclining figure — the shape of the body appears compressed and distorted, and some parts seem to disappear altogether.

Drawing a foreshortened figure is difficult at first because we find it hard to accept such distortions, which are far from the "norm". In trying to make sense of this strange, alien shape in front of us, we start unconsciously to draw the limbs and features as we *know* them to be, to try to make them more recognizable, rather than as they actually appear. The result, of course, is that the whole thing goes wrong.

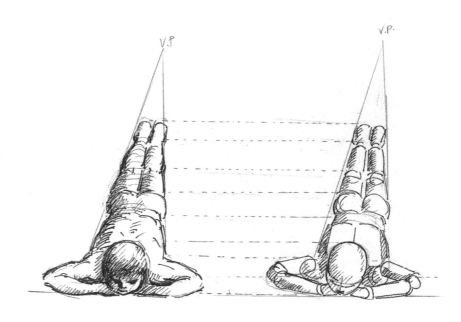

Above: Before developing detail and subtlety of form, learn to see the figure as a series of simple shapes and masses (**right**). This is a valuable tip when drawing subjects seen from different eye levels and viewpoints. This foreshortened figure, for example, can be seen as a series of spheres and cylinders diminishing in size as they move away from the viewer.

Left: When drawing the figure it helps to look carefully at the "negative" shapes between the actual solid forms of the body. Here they comprise the white spaces between the boy's legs and arms. These abstract shapes can be used to check how accurately you have drawn the figure.

If we approach foreshortening logically, however, it becomes an absorbing and satisfying exercise. Remember the underlying principle of perspective — that objects near to us appear large, while objects further away appear increasingly smaller and closer together. Therefore the part of the model's anatomy which is closest to the observer will appear larger by comparison to the part that is furthest away, for example, the feet may appear larger than the head, even though we know that the opposite is true.

When drawing foreshortened figures, you have to trust what your eyes tell you. Draw what you *see*, not what your mind tells you is correct. As you draw, constantly examine the relationship between the different sections of the body. If it helps, divide the figure into manageable sections, and use the measure-and-compare techniques described on pages 100–101.

One way of simplifying foreshortening is to treat the figure as a series of interconnecting spheres and cylinders. This makes it easier to work out which parts of the model's body are closest, and should therefore be drawn larger.

Above: As an unashamed cat lover, I have included this pencil sketch by Charlotte Halliday. It demonstrates charmingly that foreshortening applies to any figure, whether human or animal. Note how small the cat's head is in relation to the back paws. Such differences in scale can be slightly exaggerated occasionally to give greater emphasis to an interesting pose.

Right: This pastel painting by Sally Strand is a marvellous character study. The extremely foreshortened viewpoint creates impact and perfectly captures the attitude of the man slumped in a deckchair on a very hot day. The beach is a great place to make sketches of foreshortened figures – reclining sunbathers sprawl in every direction!

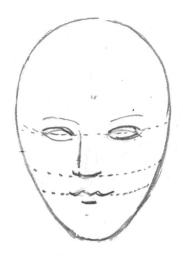

Head tipped foward
The top part of the head may appear larger than the face shape. The features are aligned within the lower half of the head.

Foreshortening heads
When the head is tipped back or forward, or when it is viewed from above or below, extreme distortions occur in the features. With the head tilted downward, for example, the eyes, nose and mouth appear compressed toward the bottom of the face and the tip of the nose may overlap the mouth. With the head tilted back, the features may appear compressed towards the top of the face, and the nose may extend above the eyes.

As with the foreshortened figure, it can be difficult to accept these distortions until we learn to look at them logically.

There is a very simple and effective piece of "equipment" which will help you to observe what happens to the features of the face when the head is tilted at various angles: it is an egg. Hard-boil it first, and then hold it pointed end down and draw a line around the middle. Now draw another line halfway below that, and a third line one-third the distance below that. Draw a pair of eyes on the mid-line, a wedge-shaped nose down to the next line, then draw a mouth on the bottom line. Turn your egg to either side and draw the ears between the lines of the eyes and the nose.

Now you have an ever-patient "model", whose head and face can be studied at leisure and from any angle.

When you look straight at the egg, the features appear proportionally spaced. Now tip the forehead end of the egg toward you: notice how the features are compressed near the chin, the top of the head appears much larger, and

Head tipped backward
The eyes and nose appear closer together. Notice how the facial features become more curved the further back the head is tipped.

Semi-profile view
As the head is turned to the side, more of the back of the head is revealed.

the ears appear much higher than the eyes. Tilt the egg back the other way; now the features gather at the forehead end, the top of the head almost disappears, and the curve of the chin is more pronounced. The ears, too, appear much lower than the eyes.

The egg model is an excellent way to understand the principles of foreshortening, but it is essential to draw from the live model, too. Observe closely as you draw, use the techniques of measuring angles and distances outlined in this chapter, and you'll soon master this challenging subject.

The head in semi-profile

When the head is viewed from a three-quarter angle the same principles of foreshortening apply, but this time in a horizontal instead of a vertical direction. When the head is turned to the side the features are aligned close to the far edge of the face. The edge of the nose, the far cheek and the far eye are compressed closer together the further the head is turned, and the tip of the nose may jut out beyond the cheek. Notice that the far eye is smaller and different in shape to the near eye. The distance from the nose to the back of the head is surprisingly long; by taking comparative measurements between the length and the width of the head you will avoid the common mistake of "squashing up" the back of the head.

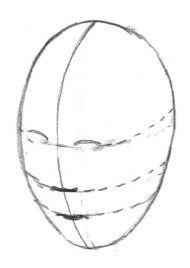

Once again your egg-head model comes in useful in understanding the position of the features. This time, draw a vertical line that passes between the eyes and down the centre of the nose and mouth to the chin. As you turn the model away from you, the position of the centre line will help you to align the features correctly.

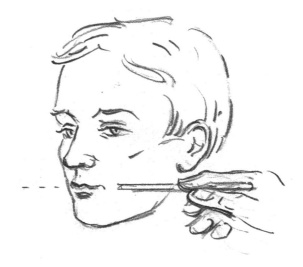

Head proportions
As you draw, use your pencil as a measuring tool to compare length to width of head and to check angles and distances between the features.

GLOSSARY

Atmosphere
In painting, ''atmosphere'' refers to the feeling of space and distance between foreground and background.

Atmospheric perspective
Also known as aerial perspective. The gradation of colours and tones to represent effects of distance and depth. As objects recede into the distance, colours appear cooler and less brilliant, and tones lighter; forms appear less distinct and tonal contrasts lessen. This phenomenon results from the fact that water vapour and dust particles in the air form a translucent veil between the eye and distant objects so that distant parts of the landscape appear bluish, their outlines blurred.

Background
The space behind principal parts of a composition that is less significant.

Blending
The fusion of tones to create soft gradations from light to dark or from one colour to another.

Camera obscura
This device, invented in 1559, was a box in which an image of a scene could be projected by means of a lens onto a flat surface. The image could then be outlined by the artist.

Cast shadow
A shadow cast by a solid object onto another object or surface, thereby revealing the direction of the light falling on it.

Colour temperature
The degree of warmth (toward red and orange) or coolness (toward blue and green) that a colour suggests in relation to other colours.

Cone of vision
Imaginary cone with its apex in the spectator's eye that defines the field of sight.

Ellipse
Ovoid shape of a circle when seen in perspective.

Eye level
In a perspective system, the height of the horizon in the picture. Anything above eye level slopes down toward the horizon, anything below it rises up to it.

Figurative
A term used to describe art that represents recognizable objects, particularly the human figure, as distinct from abstract art. Also known as representational art.

Focal point
The centre of interest in a painting or drawing.

Foreground
The part of a painting or drawing that appears nearest to the viewer.

Foreshortening
The optical distortion of forms so that they appear shortened when viewed from an end-on position.

Intensity
Refers to a colour's strength or brilliance – how vivid or dull it appears next to other colours.

Impressionism
A movement in 19th century painting originating in France in the 1860s.

Key
The prevailing tone of a picture. High-key paintings are predominantly light; low-key paintings are predominantly dark.

Landscape format
The rectangular shape traditionally associated with landscape painting, the longest edges corresponding to the top and bottom of the picture.

Life drawing
Drawing from the nude model. ''Working from life'' can be a general term for drawing and painting anything directly observed. Also known as figure drawing.

Linear perspective
The rules and conventions that govern the way objects appear to diminish in size as they recede from the spectator's viewpoint.

Modelling
The use of variations or gradations of tone and colour to achieve an impression of three-dimensional form by depicting areas of light and shadow on the subject.

Monochrome
A painting or drawing executed in one colour only.

One-point perspective
Perspective with only one vanishing point on the horizon line.

Perspective
Systems of representation in drawing and painting that create an illusion of three-dimensional depth, solidity and spatial recession on a flat surface such as paper or canvas. See also *atmospheric perspective* and *linear perspective*.

Picture plane
The vertical surface area of paper or canvas on which the artist arranges the pictorial elements to suggest an illusion of three-dimensional reality and a recession in space.

Plane
Face or surface, understood as being flat and of two dimensions (length and breadth but no depth). An object can be drawn as if it consisted of several planes or facets meeting at different angles. Also used to describe areas of a composition, such as foreground, middle ground and background.

Portrait format
The rectangular shape traditionally associated with portrait painting, the shortest sides corresponding to the top and bottom of the picture.

Renaissance
The intellectual and artistic movement that began in Italy around the beginning of the 15th century, based on reviving and re-interpreting classical Greek culture. The term comes from the French for "rebirth". The movement reached its peak during the early 16th century, in the work of artists such as Raphael, Michelangelo and da Vinci.

Scale
The size of objects in a picture relative to one another and to the viewer of the work. Scale establishes relationships between different parts of a scene and gives information about the spaces between them.

Support
Paper, canvas, board or other surface on which to paint or draw.

Surrealism
Literary and artistic movement of the 1920s and 1930s, characterized by the use of bizarre, incongruous elements.

Three-point perspective
Perspective of three planes involving three vanishing points – two on the horizon and one above or below.

Three-quarter lighting
Light that shines on an object at an angle of 45° so that about three-quarters of it is illuminated and the rest is in shadow.

Tone
The degree of lightness or darkness in a colour. Every colour's inherent tone is also modified by the effect of the available light source.

Two-point perspective
Perspective of two planes, neither of which is parallel to the picture plane, involving two vanishing points on the horizon.

Value
The quality of a tone or colour when graded from light to dark.

Vanishing point
The theoretical point on the horizon line at which receding parallel lines appear to meet.

Viewing grid
Invented during the Renaissance, this device is a transparent "window" with squares marked on it. When the subject of a painting is viewed through such a grid, it is easier to draw it more accurately and to scale.

INDEX

PICTURE CREDITS

5 Brian T N Bennett; **6–7** David Gentleman/
New Academy Gallery and Business Art Galleries;
8 Musée Condé, Chantilly/Giraudon; **9t** Scala;
9b National Gallery, London; **10t** National Gallery, London;
10b Aarhus Kunstmuseum; **11** Tate Gallery; **13** Ronald Jesty;
14–5 David J Curtis R.O.I., R.S.M.A.; **14** Betty Eberl;
16–7 Lucy Willis; **16** Geoff Humphries/Metrographic Arts;
17 Betty Eberl; **19t** David J Curtis R.O.I., R.S.M.A.;
19b Lucy Willis; **20–1** David J Curtis R.O.I., R.S.M.A.;
20 David J Curtis R.O.I., R.S.M.A.; **21t** David J Curtis R.O.I., R.S.M.A.;
21b David J Curtis R.O.I., R.S.M.A.; **22l** Betty Eberl;
22r Dennis Roxby-Bott R.W.S.; **23** Lucy Willis; **24** Lucy Willis;
25tl Lucy Willis; **25tc** Lucy Willis; **25tr** Lucy Willis;
25b Lucy Willis; **27** Ronald Jesty; **31l** Lucy Willis;
31r Hazel Harrison; **32–3** David J Curtis R.O.I., R.S.M.A.;
33 Ronald Jesty; **35** Ronald Jesty; **36** Lucy Willis;
38–9 Christopher Baker R.B.A.; **38t** David J Curtis R.O.I., R.S.M.A.;
38b Stephen Crowther A.R.C.A., R.B.A.; **42r** Roy Herrick;
43 Charlotte Halliday R.W.S.; **44tl** Michael Fairclough/
Metrographic Arts; **44tr** Michael Fairclough/Metrographic Arts;
44b Visual Arts Library; **45** William Garfit R.B.A.;
46 David J Curtis R.O.I., R.S.M.A.; **47t** David J Curtis R.O.I., R.S.M.A.;
47b Trevor Chamberlain R.O.I., R.S.M.A., N.S.; **48** Ronald Jesty;
49 Ronald Jesty; **50** Stephen Crowther A.R.C.A., R.B.A.;
51t Betty Eberl; **51b** Stephen Crowther A.R.C.A., R.B.A.;
52–3 Peter Burman/New Academy Gallery and Business Art
Galleries; **53t** Dennis Roxby-Bott R.W.S.;
53b David Carpanini/New Academy Gallery and Business Art
Galleries; **54** Dennis Roxby-Bott R.W.S.;
55 Trevor Chamberlain R.O.I., R.S.M.A., N.S.; **56–7** Lucy Willis;
56t John Martin; **56b** Stephen Crowther A.R.C.A., R.B.A.;
60–1 Trevor Chamberlain R.O.I., R.S.M.A., N.S.; **63** Jeremy Galton;
64 David J Curtis R.O.I., R.S.M.A.; **65tl** Ronald Jesty;
65tr John Newberry; **65b** Stephen Crowther A.R.C.A., R.B.A.;
67 Ronald Jesty; **68** John Newberry;
69 Trevor Chamberlain R.O.I., R.S.M.A., N.S.;
70–1 Stephen Crowther A.R.C.A., R.B.A.;
70 Stephen Crowther A.R.C.A., R.B.A.;
72 Ken Howard A.R.A., Commissioned for B.Paribas/
New Academy Gallery and Business Art Galleries;
73 Charlotte Halliday R.W.S.; **75** Keith Andrew/
New Academy Gallery and Business Art Galleries;
78 Ronald Jesty; **79** Jacqueline L Rizvi R.W.S.;
81 Jacqueline L Rizvi R.W.S.; **82** James Lee/
Metrographic Arts; **83** Jacqueline L Rizvi R.W.S.;
84t Trevor Chamberlain R.O.I., R.S.M.A., N.S.;
84b Norma Jameson; **85t** Norma Jameson; **88** Lucy Willis;
89 Lucy Willis; **90–1** Lucy Willis; **91** Lucy Willis;
92 Jane Corsellis/New Academy Gallery and Business Art
Galleries; **93** Bridgeman – Giraudon; **94tl** Joanna Wills/
New Academy Gallery and Business Art Galleries;
94tl Pandora Smith; **94b** Lucy Willis;
95 Jane Corsellis/New Academy Gallery and Business Art
Galleries; **99** Lucy Willis; **102** John Newberry;
103t David J Curtis R.O.I., R.S.M.A.; **103b** Lucy Willis;
104 John Newberry; **105l** Charlotte Halliday R.W.S.;
105r Sally Strand.